HERBERT FISHER
A Short Biography

Photo: *G. E. Houghton*

FISHER AT THE AGE OF 57

HERBERT FISHER

1865–1940

A Short Biography
by
DAVID OGG

LONDON
EDWARD ARNOLD & CO.

Printed in Great Britain by John Sherratt & Son, the St. Ann's Press,
Timperley, Cheshire.

Preface

In his preparation of this book the author has received generous help from many sources. He is specially grateful to Mrs. Fisher, to Sir Richard Burn, to Canon Spencer Leeson and to Mr. L. G. Wickham Legg, both for information and for the correction of errors, and to Mr. R. L. Rickard, of New College Library, for help with the bibliography of the subject. For the statements made and the opinions expressed the author alone is responsible.

To
MY SON

Contents

I

Birth and Parentage

THE subject of this biography was born on the 21st of March, 1865, at 3 Onslow Square, London, the first son of Herbert Fisher, who was then private secretary to the Prince of Wales. In three respects the infant was fortunate—in the period of his birth, the character of his parents, and the quality of his ancestry on both sides of the family. There was a hint of this triple felicity in the three names given to him at his christening: Herbert Albert Laurens, of which two recalled distinct elements in his natal endowment, while the name Albert, from his royal godfather, commemorated those virtues which the age held in highest repute.

In the annals of the nineteenth century the year 1865 is notable, for in that year Palmerston died, and the age of Gladstone began. With the passing of Palmerston the last, tuneful echoes of the eighteenth century were stilled; with the coming of Gladstone there became faintly audible those solemn and strident tones which now resound through the world. Statesmanship, losing its old wit and buoyancy, was about to acquire more gravity and responsibility; the blue book had already displaced the epigram; extensions of the franchise and the development of the popular Press were destined soon to create a body of public opinion before which even Parliament must bow. But the significance of these changes was not yet explicit. Coming almost exactly half-way between the end of the Napoleonic Wars and the outbreak of the first World War, the year 1865 was a good year in which to be born, for its children had nearly fifty years of peace before them, and they were never subjected to conscription; even more important, they were habituated, for the greater part of their lives, to think in terms of stability and security, progress and reform. All this was accentuated by signs of prosperity, for exports were increasing, transport was being revolutionised, and only the year before Income Tax had been reduced

9

from sevenpence to sixpence in the pound. To the poor, it was at best a leaden age, but it was the golden age of the upper middle classes, for whose sons the old public schools and a host of transformed grammar schools, many of them richly endowed with church oak and evangelical gothic, provided a discipline in religion, games and letters such as fitted them to assume the highest positions in Church and State. 'There is much that is noble in the temper of our age,' declared Bishop Samuel Wilberforce in a sermon [1] preached at this time. 'Ours is a busy, inquisitive, discovering, critical age. Labour, conflict, victory: these are its watchwords. It is a very interesting time in which to live, but it has its dangers. . . .'

Some of the dangers which the preacher had in mind are revealed in the writings of his contemporary, John Stuart Mill; indeed, between the extremes of bishop and philosopher can be discerned the broad expanse of the era in which Herbert Fisher was born. 'Who can compute,' asked Mill,[2] 'what the world loses in the multitude of promising intellects combined with timid characters who dare not follow out any bold, vigorous independent train of thought lest it should land them in something which would admit of being considered irreligious or immoral?' If the vexed philosopher had submitted this problem to the calm and dispassionate judgment of the bishop, the literary structure of the question would almost certainly have been improved, and its relevance heightened by substituting the word 'gains' for 'loses'. 'No one can be a great thinker,' declared Mill, 'who does not recognise that as a thinker it is his duty to follow his intellect to whatever conclusions it may lead.' To this Wilberforce might properly have objected that in an age when so many claimed to be thinkers the application of such a doctrine would result in anarchy—a danger from which England at least was saved by the fact that men commonly pay regard not to the profundity of a statement (which may well be a matter of dispute), but to the public or social status of the person making the pronouncement (which can be gauged by following the newspapers or consulting the reference books); moreover the divine might have added that in a true democracy such as ours, the acoustics are (providentially) so arranged that the whisper of an

---

[1] *Sermons preached before the University of Oxford, 1863–70* (1871).
[2] *Essay on Liberty* (1859), ch. 2.

archbishop carries farther than the shout of an anarchist. 'As mankind improves,' continued Mill, 'the number of doctrines which are no longer disputed or doubted will be constantly on the increase, and the well-being of humanity may almost be measured by the number and gravity of the truths which have reached the point of being uncontested.' A man of wisdom, not all of it sacred wisdom, Wilberforce might well have replied that this was over-optimistic for, in his view, as men cut themselves away from the anchorage of Christian revelation, they drift into an ocean of storm and chaos. In this respect history has justified the prelate rather than the philosopher. Wilberforce and Mill symbolised for their age the ever-recurring antithesis of acquiescence and revolt.

This antithesis was given very diverse expression in the period of Fisher's birth, and on both sides were men of genius. Already, in her *Scenes of Clerical Life* (1857) and *Adam Bede* (1859) George Eliot had stirred the placid waters of Victorian contentment, but as yet there were only ripples. Victorianism was not inspired by faith, but it was just beginning to be terrified by doubt. Tennyson's *Idylls of the King* (1859) had recalled the heroes of a primitive age, but they were gentlemanly, even devout persons, not unlike the type which the more expensive schools were striving to produce. *Tom Brown's Schooldays* (1857) had shown that, for the young, virtue is difficult; a year later *Eric, or Little by Little* seemed to suggest that it was impossible. Associated with youth in this disability were those members of the poor and the working classes who could not be described as 'deserving', for example, sea-faring men, who were credited with such depravity that a special prayer-book,[1] emphasising their 'vileness,' was published for their exclusive use. All this provided eloquent testimony of the desire to 'improve' those who were either not grown up or not respectable. In spite of Ruskin and the Pre-Raphaelites artists still commanded high prices for pictures with a moral in them, and even the sardonic Disraeli was 'on the side of the angels' (on November 25, 1864). Early in 1865 appeared the last two (of six) volumes of that biography of Frederick the Great in which Thomas Carlyle, a Scottish preacher heavily disguised as a British historian, expounded to a congregation, in which were few unbelievers, the doctrine of a solid, pious Germany, contrasted with

1 *The Sailors' Prayer-book* (1852).

an atheistic, immoral France. These things revealed a society ceasing to be quite sure of itself, but still convinced of a divine purpose in human life, most clearly evidenced by a dispensation of abundance and peace.

On the other side may be numbered the publication of *Essays and Reviews* (1860) and the incident of Bishop Colenso (1862), which for a time made the authorship of the Pentateuch and doubts about the reality of hell-fire matters of private distress and public concern. That all, except one, who had contributed to *Essays and Reviews* were clergymen of the Church of England was regarded as a sinister omen, and Bishop Wilberforce hinted, not obscurely, that as persons to whom a special measure of grace had been accorded, these sur-pliced heretics had committed the unforgivable sin against the Holy Ghost. The England of 1865 had not yet quite recovered from Darwin's *Origin of the Species* (1859), the main hypothesis of which appeared to many a blasphemous denial of divine intention, ordained for man alone, to the exclusion of what is called the brute creation; but divine intention was again ruled out by one whose influence was to rival that of Darwin, namely Karl Marx, then living precariously in Soho, who first announced himself before the uncomprehending Victorian world at a meeting of international Trades Union leaders held in London in September, 1864. From all these obscurities and perplexities there were provided a number of escape routes. Fitz-Gerald's *Rubá'iyát of Omar Khayyám* (1859) opened a pathway, through the vineyard, to the tranquil waters of hedonist agnosticism; Swinburne's *Atalanta in Calydon* (1864) offered the solace of a rare-fied paganism, while Newman's *Apologia*, published in the same year, told in prose of poetic beauty how its author had found rest for his weary head on the ample bosom of the Church of Rome.

But few Victorians can be assigned wholly to one or other of the categories implied by this antithesis, and Fisher was to prove no exception. On the one hand he was, from an early age, a sceptic of all religious formularies, and he disliked the intrigues and excesses of religious professionalism. He knew that the most insidious forms of human evil can often be concealed by the cloak of righteous in-tention, but though an adherent of no creed, he had the instinct of reverence, whether for a young child or an old church. On the other hand he had some of the qualities usually regarded as distinctive of

Victorianism, for he had a high, even stern sense of duty and honour; he believed in moral principles, in progress, in the ultimate ascendancy of the true and the good. He had a keen sense of social values; he appreciated publicity, while detesting notoriety; nor did he ever lose sight of the hair's breadth separating enterprise from adventure, investment from speculation, expediency from opportunism. Before his death in 1940 many of these convictions had been severely strained, but none of them had been shaken. If these are Victorian qualities, then Fisher was a Victorian.

To this brief selection from the intellectual influences which pervaded the England of Fisher's infancy it is tempting to add, by way of elimination, a hint of some of the differences between an environment of eighty years ago and a corresponding environment of to-day. Most obvious is the difference in speed of communication. We know that mechanical progress may exact a heavy cost in human life, but it is not so obvious that a heavier, though indirect, charge may be incurred by the changed character of life consequent on mechanical progress, since the craze for speed helps to create that restlessness which is recognised as one of the causes of international tension. Inter-state relations, once regulated by confidential and leisurely correspondence, may acquire a staccato and even peremptory character from continual resort to the telephone or telegraph; aeroplanes may bring together people who are better kept apart, and the wireless helps to maintain both a larger publicity and a heightened *tempo* in the modern crisis; indeed, the word crisis has completely changed its meaning, for whereas in 1865 it was measured in weeks, it is now measured in decades. Nor does modern science offer us any alleviation of these things, since the boundless possibilities of rocket and jet propulsion open up vistas of even faster and more spasmodic transit, so that human life which, in a remote past was said to be nasty and short, may in the near future be noisy and short. To say that these things were absent from the England of 1865 or only in their infancy is to make an obvious but vital distinction, though it is not so easy to establish deductions. One may be hazarded. We are losing the art of conversation, as we have already lost the art of letter-writing. For good conversation a certain measure of social stability and uninterrupted quiet is necessary, since only thus can it be sustained and intelligent; moreover, such conversation

is more than an amenity, it is essential in a worth-while civilisation.
Here again Fisher was blessed with one of the good qualities of his
age, for he was a brilliant speaker and talker, and (except with bores)
a good listener.

Another distinction may be suggested—a difference between our
language of 1945 and that of 1865. The English of Fisher's childhood was slightly more rotund, more ornate than that of to-day; it
was certainly more decorous. Then, as now, there were adepts in
the art of using words not to express but to conceal meaning; nevertheless, the circumlocutions of the past had usually a more literary
quality; and in mastery of this art no successor has ever approached
Gladstone. But our language now bears traces of both the inflation
and the wear-and-tear to which humanity has recently been subjected, and here we can detect an element of contrast. It is not
merely that we now have many ugly words, some foreign, derived
from the catastrophes of war and the exigencies of peace. The
change is more subtle. Thus, the simple word 'truth' is now insufficient, for we recognise distinct varieties, such as 'Protestant
Truth' and 'Catholic Truth'; moreover, we achieve higher degrees
of truth by adding words such as 'objective' or 'realistic'; nor need
we use such a stark word as 'untruth' when we have the emollient
term 'propaganda'. As words recede still further from their meaning, we are obliged, in order to carry conviction, to offer a premium
for acceptance of our depreciated literary currency by adding such
small coin as 'definitely' or 'quite definitely'. Another consequence
of this inflation is that we now lapse more easily into metaphors, so
easily that we do not trouble to maintain them, and often fail to
notice when they have become mixed. Even more, some of our most
popular similes have associations which would have been thought
distasteful by an earlier age. Thus, grants of money, formerly reserved or allocated, are now 'ear-marked'; information, hitherto
revealed or divulged is now 'released'; things in agreement with
each other are 'on all fours'; difficulties once settled are now 'ironed
out'; a scheme is a 'layout', a failure is a 'wash-out'; human beings
are 'combed out' or 'mopped up', examples which suggest that we
are becoming more dependent on the scullery and the menagerie
for our literary inspiration. At the other extreme is the use of certain
technical expressions such as 'integration' which acquire an almost

apocalyptic significance when applied to the co-ordination of social or educational reforms. This cheapening of our language is one of the differences between the English current in Fisher's youth and that prevalent in his old age. His mastery of literary English, which he shared with many of his contemporaries, was in some degree due to the fact that he was born early enough. A generation later might have been too late.

A third deduction may be suggested, based on this process of elimination. We hear much of the educational advantages of such inventions as the cinema and the wireless, and we know that the modern child is habituated from earliest years to the screen and the loudspeaker. There is difference of opinion about the possible results of such habituation, but there may be acceptance of the thesis that, in the absence of such devices, the modern family would be thrown much more on its own resources, and to that extent would be a more powerful factor in the evolution of the individual. In this way, many Victorian families, especially large ones, were more independent and self-supporting in things of the mind and spirit than is usual in the family life of to-day. The advantages are not all on one side, for in the more self-contained unit of the Victorian family certain personal characteristics might be over-accentuated; moreover, this insulation from the outside world, especially if coupled with over-rigid parental domination, might result either in rebellion or in failure to develop the qualities of initiative and responsibility. For the middle classes this danger was minimised by early residence at boarding schools, or by entry into one of the Services, in which event the family still remained as the home, the most potentially valuable, but the most seriously menaced of all British institutions. In contrast with the men of Fisher's generation, the notable men of the future will probably owe less to the home and more to other influences; many of them will be crude, forthright and dynamic, for they are less likely to have experienced the refining and restraining influences which can best be directed through the close-knit affections of family life. Fisher, on the contrary, was essentially the product of the home.

He was fortunate in his parents. His father, who had trained for the Bar and later succeeded to the Vice-Wardenship of the Stannaries (an office since abolished), was the son of a canon of Salisbury, and numbered among his ancestors bishops, scholars, bird-lovers, landscape painters, and sportsmen, 'Anglicans and orthodox and English to the core.'[1] One of them was a cousin of the poet Wordsworth. But there was a trace of French blood, derived from a Monsieur Laurens, who had come to England from Rouen in the reign of Charles II, perhaps the only adventurer in a long line of quiet-living men. The portrait by G. F. Watts suggests that Herbert Fisher senior was a thoughtful and sensitive man; his successful fulfilment of the duties of private secretary to the Prince of Wales warrants the assumption that, like his son, he was a natural-born diplomatist. He was deeply concerned for the future of his numerous children, and this sense of responsibility, amounting at times to anxiety, was shared chiefly by his eldest son.

But, like so many famous men, Fisher owed most to his mother, his 'first teacher and the best.' 'I remember your mother,' wrote a friend[2] in 1916, 'so frailly beautiful nearly fifty years ago, with you and your sister as babies. She looked like a child of fourteen then, the incarnation of grace and a kind of Botticelli beauty.' Her love and understanding were the most precious things in Fisher's young life, and in later years his letters to her reveal the depth of his devotion. She was a daughter of Maria Jackson, wife of Dr. Jackson, once a well-known figure in Anglo-Indian society, and as one of the Pattle sisters Mrs. Jackson was said to have inherited her beauty from her grandfather Antoine de l'Etang, who had been noted for both good looks and skilled horsemanship at the court of Marie Antoinette. On this side of the family, the great-aunts included Julia Cameron, a friend of Tennyson, as well as a pioneer in the art of photographic portraiture, and Sarah Prinsep, the friend of Gladstone, Burne-Jones, George Eliot, Coventry Patmore and G. F. Watts. An aunt, Mrs. Duckworth, married Leslie Stephen, whose daughters Virginia Woolf and Vanessa Bell were thus Fisher's cousins, and when it is recalled that F. W. Maitland and R. Vaughan Williams were added to the family circle by marriage with his sisters it will be seen that Fisher was no solitary genius. It was like being born in a Pantheon to which fresh celebrities were constantly being added. Eminence came to Fisher as a duty and a birthright.

This initial blessing of good family connection is sometimes

[1] *Unfinished Autobiography*, p. 6. [2] Lady Laura Ridding.

reflected in the Christian names bestowed on a child. By contrast, to have only one Christian name may imply that the journey of life has had to be undertaken with the minimum of outfit, for the solitary name, where it is not merely nondescript, may recall some old king or prophet, whom it would be impossible or unwise to emulate, and so may advertise to the world not the repute of one's antecedents, but merely the biblical preference of one's parents. Here again Fisher started with an advantage. The name Herbert linked him with his father; Albert was derived from his royal god-parent, the Prince of Wales; Laurens recalled a seventeenth-century French ancestor who, if little was known about him, had at least shown the quality of initiative. Each of these names may be taken to symbolise a distinctive strand in the pattern of the grown man. Herbert denoted the scholarly, artistic element, resulting in a refine-ment of almost feminine quality. Albert was a reminder of those virtues which had once elevated the Prince Consort to a somewhat solitary pinnacle—industry, idealism, a strong sense of public duty, and a high seriousness which allowed no place for the flippant, the indecorous or the humorous. It was difficult to live up to such an august name, but Fisher did. Laurens, a memento of the French strain in both sides of the ancestry, may be taken to describe the critic, the sceptic, the wit, always quick to detect humbug, and ready to challenge it not by frontal attack but by feint and passade as dexterous as any practised by his ancestor the Chevalier de l'Etang. These component parts, happily united, underlay a personality which, devoid of genius as of vice, was one of singular ability and grace; indeed, it was probably to the harmonious blending of these characteristics that Fisher owed his success in life.

Few, however, were sufficiently intimate to discern all the parts. The artists, scholars and musicians appreciated the humanity and connoisseurship of Herbert, always kind-hearted, though not obviously warm-hearted. For a larger public, the House of Com-mons, the electorate, the parents of undergraduates, there was Albert, almost an institution, always stimulating and high-principled, thorough and conscientious, dispassionate and olympian, but sometimes reserved, austere and aloof. To those who saw only this, the monumental side, it sometimes appeared that Fisher was built solely for large audiences. As Albert came to dominate this partnership, Laurens appears to have been kept under more strict control, and although allowed some licence at small, informal gatherings he was discouraged from making public pronouncements.

But even from this well-regulated consortium Laurens succeeded, on one occasion, in breaking loose. In 1929, for no very clear reason, Fisher, or rather Laurens, published a criticism of Christian Science entitled *Our New Religion*. It was a clever little book, so clever that it might have been written by Lucian, or Voltaire or even the Devil himself. Its effect was disconcerting. Some old friendships, including those of two prominent members of the peerage, were jeopardised; nearly as serious, the custom of the firm, particularly in the United States, was threatened with diminution, and Albert, the senior partner, may well have deplored this example of the folly of attacking a cult which has the backing of money and social influence. Indeed, for a time Fisher found himself out in the cold among the pariah dogs who bark at the sleek, pedigree creatures basking in the sunshine of popular favour. Here was the one breach in a harmonious partnership, possibly the only indiscretion in his life. But it was worth while. The blossom and fruits of maturity were the felicitous results of this grafting of a rare French bud on vigorous English stock.

II

Winchester and Oxford
1878–1888

IN 1870 Fisher's father was appointed Vice-Warden of the Stannaries, one of the offices of the Duchy of Cornwall, and he resigned
his secretaryship to the Prince of Wales, much to the regret of the
Royal Family. Residence in London being no longer necessary, the
Fishers moved first to Blatchington Court, near Seaford in Sussex,
and later, in 1878, to a house inherited by the father at Brockenhurst
in the New Forest. Meanwhile, the family was steadily increasing
and, with the birth of Edwin, the youngest, in 1883, it consisted
of thirteen persons; the parents, seven sons and four daughters, a
small community bound by strong ties of affection, and large enough
to be in many respects independent. Of the daughters, Florence,
the eldest of the family, married F. W. Maitland and, after his death
in 1906, Sir Francis Darwin, the botanist; two of the younger sisters
married musicians—R. Vaughan Williams and R. O. Morris.
Fisher's six brothers were Arthur, Hervey, Edmund, William,
Charles and Edwin. Of these Hervey was a life-long invalid; of the
others three successive wars were destined to take heavy toll. Arthur
died from the effects of his service in the South African War;
Edmund died of an illness contracted in the trenches after the battle
of Cambrai (1916); Charles, a brilliant young don at Christ Church,
perished in the same year when his ship the *Invincible* was sunk at
Jutland. In the course of that battle his elder brother William
sailed past the little wreckage that was left of the vessel in which
Charles had gone down. William,[1] who had chosen the Royal Navy
as his career, performed service of exceptional distinction, including
that of Director of Anti-Submarine operations in 1917–8, and later
as Commander-in-Chief in the Mediterranean. His premature death
at the age of 62, when he was holding the Portsmouth command,

[1] See the biography *Admiral Sir William Fisher*, by Admiral Sir William James
(1943).

was partly due to the exceptional strain imposed on senior officers in the anxious years immediately preceding the outbreak of hostilities in 1939. From the instance of this family alone, it is possible to form a dim conception of the recurrent loss sustained by civilisation through the repeated sacrifice of its best manhood.

But in Fisher's childhood, spent in an English countryside, there was no hint of these shadows. Seaford, which provided him with some of his earliest recollections, retained until comparatively recent times its character of an old borough by the sea, not yet a coast resort, because the front was undeveloped, and no longer a port, because for some geological reason the river had long ago changed its course, and flowed into the harbour at Newhaven, two miles away. But his affections were for the New Forest rather than for the Sussex coast. At Brockenhurst as a young boy he entered ardently into the activities for which there are still opportunities in the Forest, and he came to appreciate the quiet refinement which even to-day can be found in the remoter countryside of Britain. Later, he was accustomed to recommend that, for a holiday, one should go South. But he did not know the North very intimately, nor did he realise the extent of the desecration which has overtaken so much of the South.

He received his earliest lessons from his mother. Physical and mental development were unusually rapid. Riding and cricket were varied by country rambles; he was much in the society of interesting relatives, particularly those on his mother's side, and his reading was both extensive and well-selected. After a few years at a preparatory school at Maidenhead he went to Winchester at the age of thirteen (September, 1878), having missed his scholarship there through illness. He was probably right in holding, later in life, that a scholarship at what is still one of the most exacting of our public schools might have proved inadvisable, because of strain, and its possible consequence of staleness. Fisher became a good scholar at his own pace.

His House was Du Boulay's, where he was fag to Edward Grey. Between the two there developed a strong friendship, based on much common ground of temperament and, even at that age, principle. Other notable contemporaries at Winchester with whom he was later to be associated were Frederic Kenyon, afterwards

Director and Principal Librarian of the British Museum; L. A. Selby Bigge, who as Permanent Secretary of the Board of Education was one day to prove one of Fisher's ablest lieutenants, and Robert Morant, whose exceptional skill in educational administration was later revealed in the Education Act of 1902. Fisher's progress as a schoolboy was steady rather than spectacular. At his entry he was placed in the senior division of Middle Part; in September, 1881, he had risen to the junior division of Sixth Book (i.e. Form) which was taught by W. A. Fearon (who succeeded Ridding as headmaster) and Edmund Morshead; a year later he was in the senior division, under Dr. Ridding, a man whose courage and humanity served him well in a difficult headmastership, as afterwards in a difficult diocese —that of Southwell. It was he who insisted that his gifted pupil should go to New College rather than to Christ Church, in order that the link between the two sister foundations should be maintained, and at the election of December, 1883, Fisher achieved the highest distinction open to a young Wykehamist—he was placed first on the roll of scholars for New College, after an examination which, among other things, required a sound knowledge of the language and literature of ancient Greece and Rome. In the same year he won two prizes, one for Greek Iambics (a translation of Matthew Arnold's *Tristram and Yseult*), the other for a Latin essay on the subject *Architecture*, and he already had to his credit a prize in Modern Languages and the Queen's Medal for an English essay on *The insular position of Great Britain*. Thus, though not technically a scholar, Fisher was the most notable boy of his year, and one of the two or three most promising in the school.

He had not neglected the other sides of school life. Grey did not succeed in making him an angler, but his fag was a keen member of the Rifle Corps, and he played with credit in the Second Eleven, though whether he excelled in the fielding for which Winchester was then famous is not recorded, but it is certain that he retained throughout life something of the litheness and grace of the cricketer. As a member of the Debating Society he vindicated in sonorous phrases the axioms of Liberalism, whether as an advocate of Lord Ripon's policy in India, particularly the Ilbert Bill (1883), or as an opponent of the exclusion of Bradlaugh from the House of Commons (1884). On these occasions he appears to have been with

the minority, but he was with the majority when he spoke against
a proposal to abolish the House of Lords. Already, the young Fisher
was keenly interested in the public life, and he had no doubt that,
of the great political parties, the Liberal Party best embodied his
ideals. That party, under the leadership of Mr. Gladstone and before
the split on Home Rule, was then at the summit of its influence
and reputation.

Fisher afterwards recorded that he had enjoyed every moment
of his life at Winchester. The English public school does not suit
every type of character, and much of a boy's happiness and success
may depend not only on his own temperament, but on the masters
under whom he is placed and the contemporaries with whom he
has to live; moreover, a headmaster's influence may permeate, for
good or bad, through a great school. As in so much else Fisher
was fortunate in all of these things, for the Winchester which he
knew was no longer the pietistic and secluded seminary of tradition,
but a school which, while retaining much of its distinctiveness, was
rapidly being adapted to modern conditions. The boys themselves
were conscious of this change. 'Science and Modern Languages,'
wrote a contributor to The Wykehamist,[1] 'are now receiving more
attention. A Racquet Court, Gymnasium and Fives Court meet the
requirements of the age. . . . The whole of school interests are no
longer bound within the prison circuit of Meads, and a daily march
to Hills. We have Lavender Meads and New Field and country
walks; we have the Moberly library and School societies as well
as our school work; and what perhaps makes more difference than
all, less remoteness between Master and Boy.' But, in the opinion
of this youthful contributor, there were some serious faults. He
detected a new spirit of 'snobbishness' and 'offensive personalities'
at football matches. He complained also of 'swindling' practised
'up to books' (i.e. in class). Another contributor deplored the 'jaw-
ing' among both football players and spectators. Possibly the school-
boys of those days were more reticent or more subdued than their
modern prototypes.

Fisher owed much to Winchester. He had entered it a shy,
somewhat overgrown boy of thirteen, of wide reading and undeveloped interests; he left it six years later an accomplished classical

[1] October, 1822.

scholar, a good linguist, a ready and effective speaker, a keen student of contemporary affairs. In congenial surroundings he had developed his natural bent; the *venustas* of school and cathedral city accorded well with his instinct for all that is graceful in the legacy of the past; and in the humanities, using that word in both its most exacting and most liberal sense, he was exceptionally well endowed. He noted only one defect in the equipment provided for him—the absence of natural science. For the historian this is usually considered superfluous. But he remained conscious of the deficiency, and he may have been right in thinking that a historian, completely ignorant of those great sciences to which so much of the best human intellect has been devoted, is not fully equipped for his task.

The Oxford to which he came in October, 1884, as a Winchester Scholar of New College was one of the last of our national institutions to experience the stirring winds of reform; indeed, it may be said that only in consequence of these reforms had Oxford and its colleges come to be considered national institutions at all. Of this change New College provides a good example. Originally founded, on a scale which in the fourteenth century was sumptuous, for a community of seventy persons, drawn from Winchester, a portion of whom were Founder's Kin, the College in 1854, when reforming began, was, in Fisher's words,[1] 'contracted, indolent, orthodox and obscure.' It was then one of the smallest of Oxford colleges, its intake from Winchester amounting on an average to only five or six persons per annum, all of whom had been nominated to a Fellowship on the foundation at an age when, in modern conditions, they would be candidates for scholarships by examination. Celibacy was the main condition for retention of such a Fellowship, and a benefice in the gift of the College was the usual object of ambition, for this provided a competence on which the penurious ex-Fellow could marry. The College had in fact shrunk into an annexe to the Established Church, and not even a satisfactory annexe, because there was little incentive either to study or teaching, mainly because, by ingenious perversion of mediaeval statutes, the Fellows had long enjoyed the privilege of obtaining their degrees without examination. Nor was there any preparation for the parochial duties which for most of the foundationers provided the inevitable career. The

[1] *Unfinished Autobiography*, p. 43.

revenues came mainly from the lands of the original endowment, most of them let not at a rack rent but held on beneficial leases, with a fine on renewal, and so the connection of the College with its agricultural tenants was less intimate than it is to-day.

But, though so badly in need of reform, few colleges adapted themselves so quickly to the changed conditions, and almost from the outset the College (by a majority) acquiesced not only in drastic alteration of its own constitution, but in those wider schemes intended to ensure the appropriation of a portion of college revenues to university purposes. Even before the commission of 1852-4 the College had decided to substitute examination in place of nomination of the scholars from Winchester, and to admit Commoners, from whatever school, provided they passed the College entrance examination, and showed themselves capable of reading for an Honours degree. This extension was further facilitated by the Act of 1871 which removed religious tests as a condition for degrees, except in the Faculty of Divinity. The result was that in the twenty years following the legislative changes effected in 1854-6, the College increased its membership to about 200, and took its place as one of the most progressive colleges in the university. Moreover, the contribution of its surplus revenue to the university brought its association, first, with the Savilian professorships of Geometry and Astronomy and, later, with the three Wykeham professorships of Logic, Physics and Ancient History, all of which added considerable intellectual distinction. Later changes, such as those advocated by the Commission of 1877, increased the number of open scholarships, and, by relieving the condition of celibacy, have enabled Fellows to take up College teaching as a career.

These things are familiar to those who have experience of the Oxford or Cambridge system, but they may seem mystifying to those who know only the Scottish, or the Continental, or the modern English universities; for in all of these the professor or university lecturer is the teaching unit, and his students usually include all the members of the university who are taking his subject. But this is not true of Oxford to-day, and still less of the Oxford of 1884. The system, now a dual one, was once almost an antagonism—between university on the one side and the colleges on the other, the one represented by professors and lecturers, the other by fellows and tutors. In 1884 the University of Oxford was a poorly-endowed corporation, receiving no government grant, dependent mainly on fees paid by graduate and undergraduate members of colleges, and obliged to maintain, among other things, a church, a library, several museums, a botanic garden and a park. An examining and degree-conferring body, it was only beginning again to be a teaching institution, for its professors, though mostly distinguished, were comparatively few in number, they were not well paid, they had meagre audiences, and some college tutors even discouraged the attendance of their undergraduates at professorial lectures.

In contrast, some of the colleges were richly endowed and, owing to the more limited number of subjects taught, even the poorer colleges could usually provide from the Fellows whom it had elected all the teaching required for its undergraduate members. Except for the comparatively small proportion taking scientific subjects, the Oxford student need never even see a professor, nor was he likely to think of the university as a teaching body at all. This distinction is not merely one between two different types of institution, but between two radically opposed conceptions of higher education, an antithesis most clearly in evidence at the time of the Commission of 1852–4, and not yet completely eliminated from English academic life. To many university reformers of the mid-nineteenth century Germany, especially Prussia, was the ideal to be followed. It was unquestionable that in elementary and secondary education the Prussian model was one of thoroughness and efficiency; moreover, at the universities were the German professors, with their enthusiastic audiences, and their renown (especially in England) for exacting scholarship; while for research, there were innumerable seminars and laboratories, devoted not merely to the teaching of the young, but to the discovery of new truths. All this contrasted to the disadvantage of conditions in England, where there was no national system of elementary education, where the two older universities, ignored by the State, were overshadowed by numerous colleges which, in their monopoly of the student's academic life, kept him from the few and obscure professors provided by the university, closely supervised his moral conduct, limited him to the tuition given by college tutors, and regarded research with indifference and even contempt. The balance seemed to weigh so heavily towards the Continental example that Dr. Pusey, in his evidence before the Commission of 1852–4, showed some courage in questioning the alleged superiority of the non-residential, professorial university to the residential, tutorial college. Speaking from experience of German universities, he went so far as to suggest that many German professors, particularly of Theology, were charlatans, enjoying reputations built up for them by large, sheep-like audiences, whose education consisted in laboriously writing out versions, often garbled, of such pronouncements from the lecture platform as reached their ears.

Nor was this all. The redoubtable Dr. Pusey went so far as to claim that with the invention of printing professorial lectures had become obsolete. He excepted the sciences, where lectures may be accompanied by demonstrations; but in Arts and Divinity he contended that a series of lectures, even if accurately taken down, is usually inferior to the printed book. Moreover, according to Pusey, in lands where professors are held in high repute, religious beliefs may be undermined by the succession or rivalry of 'schools' of theology, each intent on capturing the largest following by discrediting its competitors, and in this way some of the academic products of such traditions may be a far more serious menace to faith than the atheist or agnostic, since they can often 'prove,' on the best professorial authority, that many things regarded as fundamental are really myths. In this crusade Pusey went far, but some of his less-known contemporaries went farther, and singled out for condemnation even the University sermons, preached at regular intervals by select preachers (including Dr. Pusey himself) whose views, it was thought, were unsettling, since so few preachers seemed to agree on the same things. Abstention from such functions, together with regular and choral celebration of Holy Communion, and avoidance of all places of worship likely to be frequented by the other sex, such was the recommendation of one College tutor, anxious to safeguard his charges from the triple peril of professors, preachers and women.[1] History was adduced in order to prove that the colleges had been instituted on a semi-monastic basis, in order to struggle with the 'monster evils' of the university.[2]

[1] *Spiritual Destitution at Oxford.* A Letter to the Bishop of Oxford. By a Fellow of a College (1876).
[2] *Ibid.*, quoting from *Christian Schools and Colleges*, II, 259.

When in October, 1884, Fisher went to Oxford this antithesis still survived, but it was much less acute. Public opinion had gone against Dr. Pusey, and professors had come to stay. The University of Oxford then consisted of about 2,000 resident members, mostly housed in about a score of colleges and halls, under the nominal headship of the Chancellor, Lord Salisbury. Of about fifty professors, some were men of great distinction, notably Stubbs (Modern History), Bryce (Civil Law), Dicey (English Law), Nettleship (Latin), and Ruskin (Fine Art). But, with the exception perhaps of Ruskin, it may be doubted whether even these men had much influence on the undergraduates, and indeed Stubbs complained bitterly of the fact that he had to deliver his lectures to small and unrepresentative audiences.

Fisher's unfailing good fortune followed him to his Oxford college. New College was then a society of about two hundred resident members, of whom twenty-five were fellows, forty-two scholars, and the remainder commoners. An organist, with eight lay clerks and sixteen choristers, was responsible for maintaining the high musical traditions of the college, and a schoolmaster presided over the choir school. The warden was Dr. J. E. Sewell, still affectionately remembered by an older generation, who in his placid forty-three years of office (1860–1903) witnessed a great many changes, in some of which he acquiesced, while of the others he became too deaf to realise the full significance. Of the fellows, the senior was Founder's Kin, the last survivor of a troublesome set of men. The personal link with the University was represented by the two Savilian professors of Geometry and Astronomy, Sylvester and Pritchard. Alfred Milner, afterwards Lord Milner, one of the old non-resident life Fellows, was already showing how academic distinction could be combined with a high standard of public service. The removal of religious tests was exemplified by the presence in the same society of Croke Robinson, afterwards domestic chaplain to the Pope, and R. F. Horton, who was to prove a leader of English Nonconformity. Finance and estate management were in the hands of Alfred Robinson, whose wise administration guided the College skilfully through a period of radical change. Of the remaining Fellows, eight were actively engaged in teaching. Hereford B. George was a pioneer in alpine climbing and in the collegiate teaching of

27

Modern History; W. A. Spooner (afterwards warden) combined the office of Dean with teaching in Divinity, Classics, and Philosophy, of a type sometimes unconventional and never highly specialised, while beneath an appearance of venerable old age (he was then forty) and a grossly exaggerated reputation for verbal eccentricities, he concealed a singularly astute knowledge of men and things. Law was taught by J. B. Moyle, an outspoken man, whose quality of sarcasm was more direct than that of Spooner; in contrast with Moyle was the retiring and diffident Hayes, whose subject was Mathematics. Prickard, a fine scholar and athlete, always genial and courteous, shared the teaching for Honour Classical Moderations with D. S. Margoliouth, whose knowledge of Latin and Greek was equalled only by his scholarship in Hebrew and Arabic. Margoliouth was then a formidable man, but he mellowed with years. For most of the teaching in 'Greats,' W. L. Courtney and P. E. Matheson were responsible, the former in Philosophy, the latter in Ancient History. Courtney, in appearance more like a dragoon than a don, was a handsome and versatile man, who afterwards forsook the academic life for journalism. Matheson remained to devote his solid wisdom and exacting solicitude, to the best interests of college and university. It will be seen that the teaching provided was rather less varied than that provided to-day, being limited mainly to the older Art subjects, but that it was generally of very high quality there can be no doubt. Margoliouth alone had enough erudition to stock a whole university (not to speak of a college), if science and economics be left out of account.

Fisher has recorded that his undergraduate career at Oxford was not one of the happiest periods of his life. He contracted jaundice in his first term, and he suffered from a strained heart, the result, he thought, of football at Winchester; moreover, the Oxford climate did not appear to suit him. As the eldest son of a family large even on nineteenth-century standards, he was acutely conscious of the fact that, in spite of his scholarship of £80 a year, he was still, to some extent, a financial burden on his parents. These things may have combined to make him something of a valetudinarian, though he was never a faddist, nor even an ascetic. But he was careful of himself; his habits were abstemious; he did not smoke, he took regular but moderate exercise, and his health, never robust, but always carefully conserved, was of that even tenour which is often compatible with sustained efficiency and long life. Some years later he suffered from stone, and his digestion was delicate, but it was noted that, after his visit to India (in 1913) his general health improved. At the age of seventy he recovered almost completely from a serious breakdown, the most striking proof of his well-preserved store of nervous and physical reserves. If health be a factor in mentality, then it may be said that Fisher's equanimity, his avoidance of extremes, his distrust of the emotional and the headlong were all linked with a life-long regime which conserved his physical and mental powers.

For the greater part of his first two years at Oxford he was engaged in study for Classical Honour Moderations. The course, which can profitably be taken only by those who already have a good knowledge of Latin and Greek, involved an extensive and critical knowledge of the greatest of the Latin and Greek authors, as well as ability to do prose and verse compositions. In this way, the linguistic and literary training of Winchester was continued on a more intensive scale, and Margoliouth induced him to devote the greater part of a term to the study of Persian. In March, 1886, his name appeared among those who had been awarded First Class Honours in Classical Moderations, and he then commenced the study of Philosophy and Ancient History, in order to take the final School of Literae Humaniores, or 'Greats,' usually completed in two years and a term after Moderations.

The Oxford 'Greats' School still retains its high repute as the best of the Arts courses; indeed, it is unique. Based on the critical study of classical texts in the originals, it is in effect limited to those who have been taught Latin and Greek at school. But, as it is somewhat more elastic than Classical Moderations, a First Class is open to men of different types of ability or interest; moreover, the course, providing as it does an intensive study of ancient thought and civilisation, is often the best preliminary to the pursuit of other subjects, particularly Modern History, and not even excluding Physical and Chemical Science. Not unnaturally, 'Greats' is taken by the best Arts students (in spite of substitutes which provide for study of translations), whatever may be their ultimate goal, because in no other way can the critical sense be so highly trained, nor can the European heritage be properly valued unless account is taken of the legacies of ancient Greece and Rome. Bishop Stubbs was by no means alone in thinking that a First in 'Greats' is a better qualification for the study of mediaeval and modern history than a First in the School devoted solely to these subjects, and Fisher himself, who never took the School of Modern History, is a striking confirmation of this view. But there are imperfections in even the best of human things. One is that the course in fact, though not by any formal regulation, is limited to those who have had a sound training in Latin and Greek at school. The second is that a youth, starting with this, usually a class advantage, may, merely as a good examinee, obtain the coveted First in Greats. But he may be a mediocrity nevertheless, sustained throughout his academic life by the repute of his university, his subject and, sometimes, his college.

As a 'Greats' student, Fisher in the second part of his academic course (1886–8) was a pupil of Courtney and Matheson. He was profoundly influenced by certain books. It was the period when Oxford philosophy was dominated by the teaching of T. H. Green, whose *Principles of Moral Obligation* and *Prolegomena to Ethics* habituated their readers to associate metaphysics with ethics, and to regard dialectic not as an end in itself, but as a means of formulating wise principles of conduct. Philosophy, as with Plato, was linked with the good life, with personal and social purpose. It is a testimony to this influence that Fisher was attracted more by the philosophic than by the historical side of 'Greats,' and indeed he had thoughts of devoting himself to the study and teaching of philosophy. This bent can be traced in his historical writings. It led him to value facts not in themselves, but as illustrations of movements or principles; it induced him to distinguish clearly between history and antiquarianism, and still more, it enabled him, in wide surveys of human activity, to take the long view in preference to the short-term interpretation which judges only by immediate results. It saved him from the two extremes which beset the historian —the arid and the meretricious. But why did he forsake philosophy for history? The answer is probably that he connected principles with practice, and he may have been alienated by an increasing tendency, obvious even in his own day, to indulge in distinctions without differences, to resort to the safety of mere negativism, to pull up weeds in other people's gardens, even when the other people protested that the weeds were not there. Fisher never lost his love for philosophy, but he had no patience with mere verbal ingenuity.

Meanwhile, he had to think of a career. Would he follow his father's footsteps and go to the Bar in the hope that he might one day have a practice? Or would he remain in Oxford on the chance of securing the modest but immediate income of a don? His First in 'Greats' in the summer of 1888 and the offer by New College of two fellowships to be filled up by competition decided him. In October, 1888, he was elected, after examination, a Winchester Fellow of New College, the successful candidate for the other fellowship, open to all graduates, being Gilbert Murray of St. John's, the ablest of the younger classical scholars in the university, if not in the kingdom. Thus began Fisher's career as a teacher, and his life-long friendship with one of the most notable men of his time.

III

The Oxford Don
1889–1912

THE Prize Fellowship of £200 a year for seven years offered possibilities which Fisher keenly appreciated. He was not bound to teach; he did not even have to be permanently resident in Oxford, and he could regard the Fellowship as intended to help him prepare for a learned profession, whether academic or not. The offer of such wide opportunities is now more rare, for endowments of this kind, as they are usually given to persons who have qualified themselves for a definite piece of research, are more closely identified with the academic life or, as sometimes in science, with the industrial world; whereas the earlier type of prize Fellowship might enable a man of intellectual promise to enter some form of public service, and the example of Lord Milner alone is sufficient to attest the possibilities inherent in the older system. Hence also it was more difficult for Fisher to make a choice. He had not even decided on a subject. He had rejected Philosophy; his second choice might have been Classical Archaeology, but these were the days before the discoveries of Sir Arthur Evans in Crete had revolutionised the subject. Keenly interested in public life, he felt the need for studies having a direct bearing thereon, and his choice of Modern History for this purpose may have been determined in different degrees by his friendship with three remarkable men, two of them related by marriage, who were influencing him at this most receptive and critical part of his career, namely, Leslie Stephen, F. W. Maitland and F. York Powell. Stephen, who had renounced his Holy Orders and his Cambridge Fellowship, was then engaged mainly in journalism of a very high order; Maitland was afterwards Downing Professor of the Laws of England at Cambridge; York Powell was then a very unconventional Law tutor at Christ Church. That Fisher the agnostic and philosopher was transformed into Fisher the historian and man of affairs by the instrumentality of an ex-clergyman and two lawyers is a tribute not only to the kaleidoscopic variety of English intellectual life in the later decades of the nineteenth century, but to that absence of excessive specialisation which often produced such happy results in the past.

This apparent paradox is partly explained by the fact that Stephen and Maitland, though not known as metaphysicians, were each interpreting the past from the point of view if not of the philosopher, then of the thinker. It is this quality which gives to Leslie Stephen's *English Thought in the Eighteenth Century* its unique place in our literature, for it links, as does no other book, the essential qualities of the eighteenth century with the evolution of its abstract thought, and so the period of Jenkins's Ear and the Boroughmongers becomes one of absorbing interest to those students of history who are interested in men's minds. So too his *Hours in a Library* provides graceful witness of that older scholarship which knew no barrier between history and literature. This instinct for free enquiry into questions of the present and the past, unhampered by the conventional distinction of subject, and enhanced by a prose style always attractive and understandable, provided the main link between Fisher and Leslie Stephen; they had also in common a love for the open air and a hatred of obscurantism. Like his contemporary Andrew Lang, Leslie Stephen provided stimulus rather than direction, curiosity rather than satisfaction, and their weaker disciples (if they had any) were likely to suffer from diffuseness and dissipation of effort. From this danger Fisher was saved by the stern moral fibre of his character.

If a philosopher can be defined as one who is interested in pieces only as parts of a whole then F. W. Maitland was a philosopher. To him a genealogical tree, a pronouncement by a thirteenth-century judge, a Record Office deed, or an impatient ' aside ' by a monkish chronicler, these things were among the innumerable details which he regarded of value not in themselves but as links in the piecing together of the fabric of an extinct civilisation. It was natural that, for this purpose, he should depend mainly on legal material; indeed, it is just because conveyances and enfeoffments are intended to be preserved that mediaeval archives are so rich in these things, and together with the Year Books they provided Maitland with the dry bones from which he created something with the quality of life. From the laborious collation of scattered evidence, by a process of reasoning from the known to the unknown, he was able to reconstruct much of the social and legal texture of England in the Middle Ages, and this in a literary style which gave to the subject a new element of fascination, for he was a researcher with a keen sense of humour, and his sallies of wit are often flashes of insight, directly arising from his handling of a theme. Maitland combined scholarly exactitude with vivid imagination—a very rare alliance. It is not surprising that he induced his brother-in-law to devote himself to the study of history, particularly mediaeval history. Both were agreed that history should be a record of facts, as truthful as possible, but (an important proviso) that it should be an intelligent and readable record, the result not only of research but of reasoning, tinged unmistakably with the personality of the writer. History from this point of view was not a scientific system but an intellectual adventure.

York Powell, the third member of this trio, was one of those men whose personal influence is much more important than their published work. A product of the combined Law and History School which had served a good purpose in the period 1853-73, he was known to the outside world for his knowledge of Icelandic literature, and to Oxford as the most cosmopolitan of its many eccentrics. His reading, like the company he kept, was more indiscriminate than that expected of a don, ranging from remote Venetian treatises on statecraft to the weekly literature provided for juveniles and the unsophisticated; indeed, he was more interested in men than in books. His appointment in 1894 as Regius Professor of Modern History at Oxford was due solely to intelligent selection made by the Prime Minister, Lord Rosebery (an old pupil), and it can well be understood that his inaugural lecture, lasting only half an hour, proved disappointing to those who felt that such brevity was both unacademic and unseemly. Moreover, this lecture contrasted most unfavourably with the famous inaugural delivered in the following year by Lord Acton, on his installation as Professor at Cambridge—another personal selection of Lord Rosebery's, but this time it was the leading favourite, in contrast with the rank outsider of the year before, when 'inside' knowledge had determined the choice. A big, bearded man, York Powell stampeded through the sacred enclosures

of donnery, a source of inspiration to the intelligent and of indignation to the conventional. He was heretic enough to reject the contemporary adulation of the erudition and scientific accuracy of the
German historians, and he even believed that a young scholar had
better go to Paris than to Berlin. Fisher, like so many of the best
of his generation, had come under his spell, and the advice that
he should continue his studies in France accorded with his own
preferences. So in October, 1889, having completed his statutory
year of residence, he went to Paris.

That the choice was sound was shown by the list of teachers
whose lecture courses he attended. These included Bémont, for
mediaeval history; Sorel, for the French Revolution, and Lavisse,
mainly for the seventeenth century. But he met many distinguished
Frenchmen outside the lecture-room, joining in the sparkling conversation at the salon maintained by the ebullient Taine, and hearing from the lips of the great Renan words of pessimism about the
future of France. At the Ecole des Chartes he obtained an introduction to Palaeography, and in the example of Fustel de Coulanges
he saw how a scholar could successfully apply a knowledge of the
ancient world to problems of modern times. He met Charcot, the
physician and psychiatrist, who advised him to pursue a three years'
course in Medicine before attempting to pass judgment on the
personalities of history. To all this Fisher was acutely sensitive, for
he was profoundly impressed by personal contact with some of the
most intelligent men in France, a France not yet fully recovered
from the tragedy of 1870, and still apprehensive of the stability of
the Third Republic. Throughout life he maintained many friendships with French men-of-letters, including Elie Halévy, whose
Histoire du Peuple Anglais au Dix-Neuvieme Siècle is one of the
few examples of sustained and effective history writing yet produced
in this century. Moreover, the French influence, like the French
strain in his ancestry, was destined to permeate Fisher's historical
work, serving to distinguish it from English, and still more from
German models, for he was induced thereby to associate literary
production with the *magnum opus* of the man of genius rather than
with the monograph of the archivist or researcher. In this way the
influence of Maitland and York Powell was reinforced by the
example of the greatest historians of France, and already he was

turning to two subjects worthy of the ambitious historian—the Mediaeval Empire and the French Revolution, blissfully unaware of the fact that he was probably the last man of ability to think of doing adequate justice to subjects so vast, so different and separated by such a stretch of time. This broad and ambitious approach to history recalled the eighteenth century rather than the nineteenth.

Fisher's activities in Paris were not limited to the Sorbonne and the Ecole des Chartes, for he soon got into touch with the artist community, and there he began a life-long friendship with William Rothenstein, then a student at Julian's. The late Sir William Rothenstein recorded the following recollections of this period:

'Fisher's company was a notable addition to our small circle. His enthusiasm for anything that he found exalted in literature, his readiness to admire, with us, the bridges, the river, the old streets and the varied life of Paris made him an ideal companion. He listened to our newly-found enthusiasm for the *plein-air* painters, then fashionable among the more adventurous students. Fisher, who had been brought up in the society which gathered round Watts at Little Holland House, lovers of the grand manner of the Venetians, of a rich subject matter appropriate to the ample Victorian interiors, made a gallant effort to follow us in our worship of new idols. In the Palace of Art at the great Exhibition of 1889 was a vast assembly of contemporary paintings, but we had eyes only for the 'moderns,' whose preoccupation with sunlight effects on figure and landscape seemed then of exciting significance. Fisher now declared himself a convert to impressionism. He wished, too, to see for himself the ways of a Paris studio, and came with us one morning to Julian's, and tried hard not to be embarrassed at the sight of models of both sexes, and at the noisy reception of a stranger.

'None of us proposed to accompany him to the Sorbonne, but when he went to the receptions of the great, we stayed up late to await his return, when he gave us glowing accounts of the men he had been meeting, and of the fine talk he had listened to. If Fisher learned something from us of the ways and outlook of painters, he infected us with his admiration of French learning and literature. . . . But, since leaving Paris, his loyalty was again given to Watts, though he was ever ready to listen to others, and to respect the work of others, whose qualities were pointed out to him. He was puzzled, as were many others, by the paintings of his cousin Vanessa Bell and her friends, though he greatly admired the literary gifts of her sister Virginia Woolf.'

Few things are more characteristic of Fisher than this sympathetic toying with the Impressionists and his return to the school of G. F. Watts.

The summer term of 1890 was spent in Oxford, where he lectured on Plato and took the morning roll-call. In the autumn he again went abroad, at first to the University of Göttingen, where he spent the greater part of the winter, and then to Dresden and Weimar in the spring of the following year. His knowledge of the language, as well as facilitating conversation, enabled him to study the economics of mediaeval Germany, and he read widely in German literature, notably in Goethe. He was deeply interested in German history and letters, and like most of his English contemporaries he went to Germany not to criticise, but to admire. Nevertheless, in spite of his patience and tolerance he was conscious of an impression very different from that experienced during his stay in France. Some educated Germans he liked, but others he found naïve and credulous, individually polite, but collectively arrogant, showing already the influence of Treitschke who, even more than any of his fellow-publicists and historians, was assiduously preaching two things—hatred of Great Britain and Liberalism, and glorification of 'total' war, when waged by Germany. That perfidy and brutality on a massive scale should be preached not by a gangster but by a professor was a sinister thing, recalling Hobbes's distinction between 'barren evil' and 'fertile evil': the one obvious, limited and objective, affecting only a small proportion of one's contemporaries, and ending with the death of the malefactor; the other subjective and imponderable, always respectable and often idealist, a growth outlasting the span of human life, extending its poisoned fruits to generations of men. Of these things Fisher was only faintly aware. He never lost his love for the great literature and music of the older Germany, but he did not share the admiration expressed by some of his English contemporaries for the virtues of that state which Bismarck created and Treitschke inspired.

Meanwhile he had made up his mind that his immediate vocation lay in the study and teaching of Modern History, and his Prize Fellowship provided him with a basis for this ambition. His College had no hesitation in adding him to its teaching staff, and so, soon after his return from abroad, he was appointed by New College tutor and lecturer in Modern History, an office which necessitated residence in Oxford (with vacations on a generous scale) and the performance of multifarious duties. As a Fellow of the College he was one of the governing body, and so was able to familiarise himself with the details of college administration. As lecturer he had a double set of duties—lecturing, usually twice a week during two terms out of three to audiences not limited to members of his own College, and ' tutorial ' or individual teaching of those members of the College who were reading for the final School of Modern History. This latter duty was the most substantial of all, and to it alone were devoted about eighteen hours per week. Each pupil brought and read an essay on a prescribed theme, the reading lasting for about a quarter of an hour, and then the tutor discoursed on the subject, with special reference to the essay, for the remainder of the hour. As the pupils represented each of the three years of normal residence, the teaching might have to cover a great variety of subject—the Anglo-Saxon period, the Tudors, the mediaeval papacy and empire, the age of Napoleon, the eighteenth-century enclosures, the financial achievements of Mr. Gladstone, not to mention Political Economy and Political Science. Such is not an unfair sample of the diversity of an average week's teaching. There was similar range in the intelligence of the pupils. One might be a youth of obvious intellectual powers, whether a scholar or commoner; another might be of that type, now less common, which came to the university as part of a social career, and regarded tutor and subject with well-bred tolerance. The majority came somewhere between these extremes.

The tutorial system has long divided the opinions of observers. It may first be objected that it is wasteful, because there is little division of labour, one tutor, in many colleges, being responsible for practically all the subjects in a final Honours School. Nowadays there is more specialisation than was possible in Fisher's time, for there is often an interchange of pupils with other colleges, and mediaeval history is becoming as distinct as ancient history, having its own technique and its own teachers. The objection of wastefulness might also be urged on financial grounds. The tuition fees paid by the undergraduate—a very small part of his total expenditure at the university—are insufficient to provide more than a fraction of the modest salary paid to the tutor, and the balance has to be made up from College endowments. Hence a certain disproportion between the time and money devoted to the teaching of an Oxford or Cambridge Arts undergraduate and that spent on similar students at other universities, where in place of the college endowment there is the State grant. Nor is this all. As branches of the subject, such as the history of the United States or Economic History, become popular, university professors are appointed to lecture on such subjects, but undergraduates cannot always be induced to attend their lectures, and develop the habit of depending on the omniscience of their college tutors for personal instruction in subjects of which the tutors may know little. A college don, keen on the progress of his pupils, because of his personal and almost always friendly relations with them may have to sacrifice time which otherwise might be devoted to study or research, a sacrifice less likely to be demanded of the professor, who usually knows his pupils only as members of an audience. Except in science and medicine, university teaching, as distinct from college teaching, has not yet become an integral part of the Oxford undergraduate's life, and it has to be recalled that, save for his brief tenure of the Vice-Chancellorship of Sheffield, Fisher was never in the permanent and direct service of a university. To some, indeed, it would appear that the normal and traditional type of university, as known in Scotland and on the Continent, has never been acclimatised in England at all.

But Fisher experienced the tutorial system when it was probably at its best. Among his pupils were many of those who do well, whatever the tuition; students who can stimulate even an able teacher with some unexpected or well-maintained point of view, and can also profit by the older man's balance and experience. With such pupils Fisher was at his best, for like all natural-born teachers he responded readily to the give-and-take which underlies real teaching. For the completely indifferent or idle, his icy manner would cause a distinct lowering of the temperature of the room, and to that extent at least he was a deterrent to the casuals. The average pupil, awed at first by his tutor's dignity and reserve, would quickly gain a new, and usually more intelligent, interest in the subject as Fisher discoursed on the essay, mingling criticism with encouragement, and illuminating the topic, however specialised, with analogies or contrasts drawn from a vast range of historical knowledge, so that what had appeared at first to be remote or detached became linked with the broad stream of human development. Few of his contemporaries possessed such fertility of illustration, such ease of transit over the centuries, such acumen in eliciting the essential implications of what otherwise might have seemed of merely academic import. There have been more erudite teachers of history than he, but few can have rivalled him in spontaneity, agility, incisiveness, able to bury a legend or re-incarnate a personality with an apt allusion or a happy epigram.

He liked the hard work of teaching, and exemplified the most valuable element in the tutorial system—the personal contact which it ensures. The results of these labours are to be judged not only by the many historians whom he trained, though their number and quality alone would have justified his efforts, but also by the record of those who afterwards gave distinguished service to the State, whether as judges, or ambassadors, or teachers, or civil servants or cabinet ministers. All, in one way or another, were stimulated and guided, and some even fascinated by his teaching and influence. To make a selection of the best-known names would be invidious, and would be unfair to the hundreds who derived quite as much inspiration from one of the most effective dons of his generation. The memorial of the teacher is not in the eminence of the few who have excelled, but in the gratitude of the many who have benefited.

In the other, the less arduous, but more difficult part of his teaching duties Fisher achieved similar success. He had to give lectures to some of the most trying audiences in the world. This may need a word of explanation. Then, as now, attendance on specified lectures was recommended by the college authorities, but in the Arts course there might be several courses on the same subject, and no provision for securing attendance at any. In these circumstances the undergraduates tend to become mere lecture-tasters, willing to sample only small doses; or strict utilitarians, limiting themselves to those lecturers who happen for the time being to be examiners; or they may drift in with the large crowd which throngs the lecture-room at the beginning of term, speedily thinning out when curiosity is satisfied, leaving a small corps of veterans to whom the almost-deserted lecturer is bound to feel a certain sense of gratitude or even indebtedness. The bored, blasé, surfeited listener is by far the most difficult; by contrast, a working-class audience, or, generally speaking, a Northern or Welsh audience will often help out even the indifferent lecturer by patience or, it may be suggested, by a certain natural courtesy which prompts them to continue a course once begun. Many of Fisher's Oxford contemporaries, some of them lecturers of great ability, could attract large crowds at the start, but Fisher could retain most of his audience until the end of term, and his lectures on Political Economy are still remembered for the wide interest which they stimulated, since they were characterised not only by great powers of exposition, but by a certain force of person-ality. These qualities he retained, but in later years his public speeches sometimes lost in effect because they tended (with large audiences) to be somewhat stilted and over-ornate.

It was not long before he came to be noted as one of the younger dons for whom a brilliant career, not necessarily academic, seemed to be in store. But he felt the need of more time for research, and so he made two applications for Scottish Professorships, both un-successful. His youth may to some extent have been against him, but it has to be recalled that he was neither a member of Balliol nor a Fellow of All Souls, and therefore not, in academic opinion, in the front rank of historians. In 1894 the University of Glasgow established a professorship of Modern History and invited applica-tions. This seemed to Fisher a great opportunity, for the successful candidate would have the pioneer work of creating interest in a subject hitherto unrepresented, and this in a university at the zenith of its fame, with such professors as Lord Kelvin (Natural Philo-sophy), A. C. Bradley (English Literature) and, to Fisher most attractive of all, Gilbert Murray (Greek). There was naturally a good field of candidates. Fisher had to begin with the invidious task of collecting testimonials, a thing which he hated so much that, for the time, he may have lost his *savoir faire*. He did not ask Maitland for a testimonial on the ground that he was related by marriage; he did not consult C. H. Firth, as he was understood to be recommending T. F. Tout, nor did he approach York Powell, who was said to have written on behalf of Morse Stephens. Such scruples were rare among candidates for professorial honours. He laughingly suggested that his own pupils could testify on his behalf 'if they could write English.' His main recommendations were from Charles Bémont and Hastings Rashdall, both among the foremost of mediaevalists, but not widely known outside the ranks of scholars.

Even more invidious was the duty of making a personal call on each of the electors. In June, 1894, the candidate went to Glasgow and performed the requisite visits, but he was passed over in favour of Richard Lodge of Balliol, then a Fellow of Brasenose College. Both the visit to Glasgow and the result proved a keen disappointment, for reasons hinted at in the following letter to Gilbert Murray:

> 'I felt somehow after seeing the electors that it was more probable that they would take a narrow and illiberal view of the requirements of historical study. They seemed to be thinking of little else but the fees, and obviously wanted an Extension Lecturer rather than a Scholar. Instead of welcoming the chance of promoting historical work in Scotland, they appeared to regard the chair as a risky and improper speculation, which would hardly pay dividends, even with the most consummate manipulation of the magic lantern. However, if they take Tout or Ashley things may be not so bad. If it had not been for these odious visits, I should have enjoyed my visit to Glasgow very much indeed.'

Five years later Fisher again applied for a Scottish professorship, this time at Edinburgh, and again Richard Lodge was chosen. He was somewhat vexed to learn afterwards that as a substantial number of votes had been promised to Lodge in advance, the public invitation of applications was to some extent nominal. So ended Fisher's ambition to be a professor of Modern History. But it may be doubted whether he would have been happy at a Scottish university. Rightly or wrongly, the study of Modern History has never enjoyed in Scotland the same prestige as the scientific, classical and philosophic subjects, and though the young Oxford don would have delighted in the rough-and-tumble of the responsive and often noisy Scottish audiences, he would have deplored, in the examinations, a too faithful adherence to the *ipsissima verba* of the lecturer, and even more, the garbled versions of what, to Northern ears, his language might sometimes have seemed to imply. He would also have experienced difficulty in finding many of his students willing or qualified to embark on advanced study. Moreover, for a large part of the year he would have been cut off from the great libraries, except the Advocates' Library, and, even had he taken up the study of Scottish History, he would have found that few of the older national archives had survived the Cromwellian occupation. In these circumstances he might have been obliged to abandon the pursuit of learning and devote himself to administration.

The preceding year, 1898, had been a notable one in Fisher's life, for in that year he published, in two volumes, his *Mediaeval Empire*, the fruit of study and research, mainly in German sources, conducted during vacations, and in the two or three days a week which in term time he reserved for this purpose. From the outset he acknowledged his debt to Maitland, and in particular to Maitland's handling of philosophic-legal ideas as the best guides to the study of institutions; 'my object,' wrote Fisher,[1] 'is to examine the working of the imperial idea during that period of mediaeval history when, having assumed a definite theological shape, it operated as a powerful influence over the destinies of Germany and Italy.' The Holy Roman Empire had always fascinated him because it was an ideal embodied in a human institution, and in these two volumes he surveyed in detail that period between the ninth and the thirteenth centuries when the Empire was at the height of its prestige and power. For a gifted and enthusiastic scholar of thirty-three no subject could have been more worthy, but unfortunately this was 1898, not 1798, and Fisher did not have the backing of either *clique* or *claque*. Moreover, the subject, though on a different scale, had already been handled very successfully by James Bryce, whose *Holy Roman Empire*, first published thirty-four years earlier, had become a classic, not at one bound, but by successive and enlarged editions of what at first was no more than a prize essay. Fisher, in a manner recalling a more brilliant and buoyant age, had suddenly thrust his *magnum opus* on a world which scarcely knew his name. The book contained several mistakes of interpretation; there was some evidence of haste and even carelessness; errors and

[1] *The Mediaeval Empire*, I, p. 10.

inconsistencies had appeared in the spelling of foreign names—
these things were afterwards enumerated in an unfavourable but
gentlemanly criticism[1] which appeared in the *English Historical
Review*. Compared with Bryce's classic, Fisher's *Mediaeval Empire*
is lacking in power of narrative and lucidity of exposition; much
of it appears to be undigested, and only here and there can a trace
of promise be detected. It was his first and last venture in mediaeval
studies. It was amateurish, and much worse it was dull. As he had
failed to become a professor, so he had failed to become a mediaeva-
list.

But these disappointments were more than counterbalanced by
an event of the year 1899. On July 6 he married Lettice, daughter
of Sir Courtenay Ilbert, afterwards Clerk of the House of Commons.
Miss Ilbert, an unusually able history student of Somerville College,
Oxford, had, as an external pupil, brought essays to Fisher, and
this acquaintance, ripening into affection, resulted in their wedding.
It was to prove one of those exceptionally happy marriages, in which
there was sympathy and understanding on both sides, based on
ideals which they held in common, and rooted in a love which lasted
for life. Lettice Ilbert, a young woman of wide reading and critical
judgment, an accomplished musician and public speaker, was able
not only to appreciate her husband's life-work, but to provide friendly
criticism, in which he acquired increasing confidence. In ways more
distinctively womanly she played a decisive part in her husband's life.
She helped to take him out of the somewhat valetudinarian mood
into which he was in danger of relapsing, and she succeeded in
making him, in the best sense of the word, more a man of the world.
Much of the good health enjoyed by Fisher throughout the rest of
his life was due to her constant but never obtrusive care, and much
of his happiness he owed to this partnership, which in essentials
resembled that of his parents.

The turn of the century found Fisher established in Oxford as
a householder and, though not yet fully accepted as a historian, one
of the most noted personalities in the university. He had at least
learned the rudiments of his craft, and he now decided to devote
himself to history subsequent to the end of the mediaeval period;
and in particular to Napoleonic studies. This was to prove the main

[1] *English Historical Review*, July, 1900.

preoccupation of busy and fruitful years. In the Boer War his Liberalism placed him on the unpopular side, and this may have increased his interest in a young politician whom he had first met at the Ilberts' house in London—Mr. Lloyd George, who was then thriving on unpopularity. The Tariff Reform campaign brought him into the political arena, and as a keen Free Trader he appeared on several platforms in support of Liberal candidates. This increasing interest in politics induced him to extend still further the range of his acquaintance outside Oxford, and from the year 1901 onwards he consorted with John Morley at his house in Wimbledon, while in 1905 he had his first conversation with Lord Rosebery at his Epsom house, 'The Durdans,' where Morley was also a guest. On that occasion Rosebery expressed the opinion that Germany wanted to seize Holland, and he thought that a large proportion of the Dutch population would willingly accept incorporation in the Reich. He bitterly condemned the *Entente Cordiale* on the ground that it was foolish to attempt to isolate such a great military power as Germany, a power which, in his view, had no natural antagonism to Britain. Rosebery and Morley both expressed horror at the 'insults' levelled at the Germans by *The Times* and the *National Review*.

On another occasion Rosebery suggested that there was a lack of elasticity in British conduct of foreign policy, and Fisher was interested in his suggestion that we should adopt Napoleon's system of *Auditeurs au Conseil d'Etat*, by selecting young men of ability who would have a roving commission to travel abroad and be of service wherever there was opportunity, but he feared that the Commons would object to expenditure on such a project. In some respects the activities of the British Council have achieved this object in recent years. Commenting on his own political experience, Rosebery confessed that the Cabinet system was very haphazard, and he told how Mr. Gladstone had often introduced irrelevant topics, so that often the larger questions were not adequately discussed, a tribute to the genius of a great chairman. At another of these conversations, in September, 1909, Morley told how Haldane used to weary his Cabinet colleagues by long harangues on the contribution of Germany to civilisation. The young Winston Churchill, then coming into prominence, was favourably commented upon at these gatherings. Morley thought that he showed 'a magnificent choice of language,' though he was still lacking in deliberation, and 'doesn't understand the value of a book.' But 'he reads largely, especially on Napoleon.' In these direct ways Fisher established personal contact with the greatest of the surviving exponents of Gladstonian Liberalism.

Soon he was given an opportunity, specially valuable to the historian, of studying at first hand a particularly interesting kind of imperial problem. In 1907 the Selborne Memorandum had brought into prominence the question of a union of the South African colonies, and concrete proposals for such a union were outlined in an anonymous work, *The Government of South Africa*, published in 1908. Both memorandum and book were mainly the work of Lionel Curtis, a member, with Philip Kerr (Lord Lothian), R. H. Brand, D. Malcolm and Lionel Hichens, of the group of active and enlightened young administrators known as 'Lord Milner's kindergarten.' All of these young men were pupils of Fisher, and it was mainly through the influence of Lionel Curtis that a committee of public men in the Transvaal invited Fisher to undertake a lecture tour in South Africa in the summer of 1908. His lectures were of a general historical character, without special reference to the question of the hour, but having some bearing on the alternatives of federation or union. In Johannesburg he gave a course which included lectures on the American Republic and William the Silent; in Cape Town he discoursed on the teaching of history; at a girls' school his subject was the federation of the United States. Similar lectures were delivered in Pretoria and Cape Town. The surviving manuscripts of these lectures show that he had now fully acquired the art of exposition, and the South African Press paid tribute to the widespread interest which the lectures had aroused. On his return to England he contributed to *The Times* (October, 1908) a series of articles recording his impressions. He had found opinion divided on the question of federation or union, the Transvaal supporting the latter solution on the ground that union is both more powerful and more economical, while in the coast colonies there was a body of opinion which feared absorption. But the situation, as Fisher showed, was really controlled by the Transvaal, the richest of the South African colonies, able and anxious to help the weaker units, provided they were fused together and administered from a common source. Moreover, labour problems and the need for an efficient system of railways accentuated the necessity for union, the solution which was adopted in 1910.

In the following year, 1909, Fisher visited the United States in order to give the lectures on the Lowell foundation at Boston, and this gave him an opportunity of visiting Canada. His lectures, afterwards published as *The Republican Tradition in Europe,* were delivered to audiences which he found disappointing. 'They are quite uneducated' (he wrote to Gilbert Murray), 'and my lectures are so unsuited to them that I am abandoning my MS. and giving an improvised course.' This may be a reason why he was afterwards to prove such a success as a lecturer in the United States, for American audiences are said to prefer clever improvisations, in preference to that rigid adherence to the written text which is usual with less agile savants. His short stay in Canada, where he gave two lectures at the University of Toronto, made a more vivid impression. While he thought it not impossible that at some future date the western states of the Dominion might be absorbed by the United States, French Canada, on the other hand, 'would fight to the last man to retain the British connection.' He met Sir Wilfrid Laurier, and shared the high opinion with which that leader was regarded, but the French-Canadian politicians he regarded as 'jobbers,' pulled by ecclesiastical strings. Indeed, French Canada, with its large families, its distrust of foreign influence, its fervid ultramontanism, was of special interest to Fisher because he saw there so much that France had either rejected or outgrown, and in a characteristic paradox he declared that this part of our Empire could be best understood by a reading of St. Thomas Aquinas. He had, it is true, not read deeply in Aquinas, but that he had correctly divined the true character of the French-Canadian temperament was to be revealed, with considerable *éclat,* at a later date.[1]

But these public activities did not impede a literary output[2] of a high order, which made these first dozen years of the century one of the most productive periods of Fisher's life. His change from mediaeval to modern history, particularly the Napoleonic period, was probably due to the suggestion of Lord Acton, and was amply

[1] See *infra,* p. 131.   [2] See *infra,* pp. 142–157.

justified; but it may have meant a wrench, for the Middle Ages had never lost their appeal. In Napoleon, however, he found an almost equal source of fascination. In 1911–2 he delivered the Chichele lectures on Foreign History at Oxford, and he was already a Fellow of Winchester College, a distinction which gave him an opportunity of serving on the governing body of his old school. In 1912 his career as an academic teacher came to an end with his appointment to the Vice-Chancellorship of the University of Sheffield. He was then, at the age of forty-seven, in the full maturity of his powers and in enjoyment of a reputation which extended far beyond Oxford, where for nearly a quarter of a century he had been a College don, living in a somewhat specialised (its critics would say artificial) atmosphere, associating with men who, for the most part, were devoted to learning as an end in itself. But his contemporaries were agreed that he had an intellectual distinction, an unfailing *savoir faire*, and, if an almost obselete term be allowed, an elegance in his deportment, his literary style, his personal appearance which marked him out among men credited with a more than usual share of idiosyncrasy. He was obviously destined for high public service, but on the other hand he was a member of a profession from which the State had hesitated to draw, though the Liberal party had at least made the experiment, with somewhat ambiguous results; for while Morley and Bryce had each in turn conferred a certain dignity on the front benches, they had both finished in the Lords; and though Haldane had made his mark at the War Office with far-reaching Army reforms, he had had to face unpopularity, and even obloquy. Fisher was destined to strengthen the traditions inaugurated by these academic Liberals, and for this he had certain advantages. He was not burdened, as Bryce had been, with the title of professor; he was more nimble than John Morley; his philosophy was less abstruse than that of Haldane, and he had lived for nearly half a century without being given a doctorate. Years of academic seclusion had left few distinctive marks on him, and when a few years later his time came, it was as plain Mr. Fisher that he was accepted, without prejudice, by the British public.

IV

Vice-Chancellor of Sheffield : Royal Commission on the Public Services in India
1912–1916

IN August, 1912, Fisher wrote to Gilbert Murray announcing that he was being approached about the Vice-Chancellorship of the University of Sheffield, as successor to Sir Charles Eliot, and also that he had accepted a place on the Royal Commission to investigate the public services in India. The negotiations with Sheffield resulted in his appointment as Vice-Chancellor in November of that year, and leave of absence was given until June, 1913, so that he could proceed to India, an arrangement afterwards repeated for the period November, 1913, to February, 1914. This was not a very satisfactory scheme, and only the energy of the new Vice-Chancellor saved it from breakdown. The Fishers, with their infant daughter, moved from Oxford to Yorkshire in the summer of 1913, and after some search succeeded in finding a home at Ecclesall Hall, in attractive surroundings, situated in the suburbs of Sheffield.

The University of Sheffield is one of the youngest of our universities, its charter dating from 1905, when its four faculties were Arts, Pure Science, Medicine and Applied Science. Under the direction of Eliot the university had built up a reputation in Applied Science, notably in Metallurgy, but was still comparatively weak in other subjects. It is possibly for this reason that Fisher was chosen, but it was the very reason which some friends urged on him as a deterrent from accepting. It was also represented to him that, generally speaking, the intellectual quality of the students was low, owing, it was thought, to under-feeding or a badly-chosen dietary, and Lord Curzon, whose instincts in these matters were usually sound, questioned whether Fisher was doing the right thing in going to a provincial place so far from the metropolis. But, though he had hitherto had little chance of proving it, Fisher was a man of affairs. Provincialism had no social terrors for him, and he saw the possibilities of the new post.

C

From the outset the new Vice-Chancellor kept in view the large and enterprising industrial community served by the university, and accordingly he did not even attempt to redress the balance of subjects, but on the contrary, by personal contacts, he increased the measure of local support given to the applied sciences. He set up a Scientific Advisory Committee to direct manufacturers, experimenters and inventors to the technical literature bearing on their problems, so helping to put the industrialist in touch with the researcher and scientist. He also helped to form a delegacy for research in glass technology. Indeed, it was said of him that he visualised the university as 'a sort of power-house of the intellectual life of the diocese,' a mixing of metaphors which adequately describes this mingling of the old culture of Oxford and Winchester with the new, dynamic life of industrial Yorkshire. For this purpose he made full use of the machinery already provided by the Workers' Educational Association, and he succeeded in attracting a larger public to the orbit of the university by founding a luncheon club, in which citizens took part.

His own public addresses, especially during the earlier part of the Great War, made a remarkable appeal, and Sheffield soon began to take more interest and pride in its university. Fisher had begun from the right side—the city and the great industrial circumference.

It was not easy to harden the rarer plants to this soil, but at least a start was made. A wide range of eminent men was drawn on for public lectures, such as D. G. Hogarth for Archæology and Gilbert Murray for Greek Drama. With his genius for inducing wealthy men to show a practical interest in higher education, Fisher persuaded Sir Henry Stephenson to endow a chair of Civic Art, and he is even said to have succeeded in arousing in matter-of-fact Yorkshire minds an interest in philosophy. But for the fact that his stay in Sheffield was so short and was interrupted by two visits to India, he would have left more notable traces of his influence; nevertheless, his three years of office were such as to cause the Senate to record its acknowledgment of the great services which he rendered in every department of university life. His first administrative post was a success, to be accounted for not only by his habitual tact, energy and efficiency, but also by his obvious sincerity, and his belief in the increasingly important part which the university was destined to fulfil.

All his letters at this time reflect the joy which increased responsibility brought him. In October, 1913, after interviewing about twenty freshmen and freshwomen, he recorded that only one was fit to be in a university, 'but all were gentle and nice-mannered.' Sometimes there was a hint of irresponsibility, as when he advised his auditors 'not to be shy of rich people,' an unusual point of view which was heartily applauded. Fisher really represented an England which, in many respects, is alien to Yorkshire and the North, and, but for his absorbing interest in humanity, he might well have been a failure in his new surroundings; or rather, there were at least two Fishers, one for that glacial society where the *faux pas* is the worst of crimes, where the 'right people' are met by those who are determined to make their acquaintance, and another for the more hearty world of high teas and strong accents where, at all costs, boredom and embarrassment must be concealed. Witness his own description of two dinner-parties which he attended in the summer of 1913. The first was in the West End of London:

'Such an amusing dinner yesterday in one of the loveliest houses I have ever seen. A. J. B., Curzon, F. E. Smith, Carson, Sir William Richmond, H. G. Wells, Charles Whibley, Sir Almroth Wright, Evan Charteris, Alfred Lyttelton. The beautiful Mrs. Cust received us, but vanished before dinner to another party. I sat between F. E. and Alfred Lyttelton. F. E. very vulgar. He intends to be Secretary of State for India, and talks of no one having held that office with any vigour, etc. Alfred Lyttelton very nice. Whibley is a violent, but promising little bird, full of egotism.

There was a good deal of talk about Marconis, F. E. and Carson being unable to appear at the debate owing to their being involved in the Godfrey Isaacs case, for which the Tories round them found little excuse. They had however consulted Halsbury on the matter, and were assured that it was the right thing not to take part in the debate or division. Willie Richmond talked Italian Art and Greek Archæology. F. E. showed off on Napoleon. It is an odd crowd this lot of intelligent Tories. The house was hung round with really beautiful copies of Old Masters painted by Mrs. Cust, who has a wonderful sense of colour.'

A few weeks later he recorded this impression of a dinner with a number of mining engineers in Sheffield:

'A very intelligent, fine-looking body of men, mostly trained at Sheffield or Leeds. I sat between the chairman and old Mr. —— who is (*a*) a mining engineer, (*b*) a landed gent, (*c*) a poet, (*d*) a musical composer. A song of his ($\beta =$) was given during dinner. He's a jolly old boy, much chagrined that his last cantata was refused by the Leeds Festival. The fact is he is a mid-Victorian. I made a little speech professing a glowing ardour for mining engineering, and endured a good deal of pestilent cigar. The speaking was of a very low level, but the men were above the average, all serious, responsible fellows, and hard workers.'

Meanwhile, there was the Indian Commission. Leaving England in January, 1913, Fisher had sailed in the company of Herbert Baker, the architect, then proceeding to Delhi in order to supervise the erection of the new Government Buildings, and two distinguished Indians, Prince Ranjitsinjhi and the Maharajah of Jhalawar. Naturally, the conversation with the Indians turned on the subject of the Commission, and Ranjitsinjhi deplored what he described as an increasing lack of sympathy between administrators and people in India, partly owing to the fact that, unlike their predecessors, few of the modern officials knew any of the vernaculars. The Maharajah (one of the most enlightened of the Ruling Princes) was in agreement with this view, and he claimed that some of the higher appointments should go to Indians. 'We are a loyalist and royalist race,' he said, and he thought that a few high posts given directly by the Crown would have a great effect on public opinion. The Maharajah had two complaints—the social position accorded to Indians at English universities, and the English attitude to native manufactures in India. Of these, the first has long been a matter of controversy. His Highness deplored the fact that 'nice' society was practically closed to the native, who was thereby thrown into the company of the poor; 'and the poor,' said the Maharajah, 'are always more vicious than the rich.' Consequently, the educated Indian forms a wrong conception of England, and this he spreads abroad. As regards trade and manufacture, the Maharajah contended that the English

Government was more anxious to secure Lancashire votes than to retain India. He himself had tried in vain to revive the gold-thread industry in his native Jhalawar. Still worse, the opium grown on his territory now fetched only a tenth of its former price, owing to the convention with China, while the Chinese addicts, deprived of their favourite solace, had to resort to the even more dangerous drugs forced on them by enterprising German agents. How Fisher the Liberal reacted to these statements is not recorded.

The Commission had already set to work before Fisher's arrival in India. The Royal Commission on the public services in India, appointed in August, 1912, had for its chairman John Dickson-Poynder, Lord Islington, and included among its members Lord Ronaldshay, Sir Theodore Morison, Sir Valentine Chirol, Mr. Ramsay MacDonald, Mr. G. K. Gokhale and other distinguished Indians. Its terms of reference were to enquire into methods of recruitment and systems of training, conditions of service and salary, and such limitations as still existed in the employment of non-Europeans. This question of the further admission of Indians into the Covenanted Services, as the Indian Civil Service had formerly been called, was no new problem, and had already been investigated by the Commission of 1886-7, which had tried to mitigate the difficulty by recommending that a number of appointments set free from the Indian Civil Service should be transferred to a local service, to be named the Provincial Civil Service. This was to be recruited in the provinces, and it was earnestly hoped that its members would be accepted on a footing of social equality with the members of the Imperial Service. The Commission of 1886-7, like so many public bodies had faith in the virtues of terminology, since it hoped that Indian opinion, hitherto resentful of the name ' uncovenanted ' for the lower and native branch of the service, would accept in its place the term ' provincial,' and that this change in nomenclature would be followed by a social levelling-up. This proved a delusion.

The Commission of 1912-5, in its enquiry into the Indian and Provincial services, visited all the provinces except Assam, and occupied 126 days in the examination of witnesses. No doubt was left in the minds of the Commissioners regarding the strong feeling among Indians about the difficulties attending their entry into the Indian Civil Service owing to the fact that the examination was conducted in London, and because its subjects were such as could be proficiently studied only in Western Europe. In this respect there was a striking difference of opinion between the British and the Indian point of view. The attitude of the Commissioners was that, in the English recruitment, the competitive system had on the whole been successful, since the examination syllabus followed the curricula of the ' good schools and universities,' where there is character-building as well as study, and so the successful candidates did not usually have to undergo much special preparation. In India, on the other hand, where the universities were often no more than examining bodies, character-building did not appear to be so essential a function of education as preparation for examinations, nor did India appear to possess any ' good ' schools, though it abounded in keenly competitive examinees. The Indian attitude may have been: If I can pass an examination, what has my school or university got to do with it? Generations of educational reformers have not yet succeeded in answering this question; the Commissioners of 1912–5 could do little more than enunciate the problem. They suggested that the term ' provincial ' should be abandoned, and the name of the state substituted. They recommended also that all distinctions of public service as higher or lower should be based on work done, not on salary or race; that officials promoted from a lower to a higher service should have the same opportunities as those directly appointed; that the British preponderance in the Indian Civil Service and the Indian Police should be retained; that in education, public health and public works there should be a mixture of eastern and western, with recruitment in England and India, while in scientific and technical services recruitment should normally be in India. It was also recommended that educational institutions should be developed in order to put them on a level with those of Great Britain. These recommendations foreshadow later developments whereby a larger proportion of places in the Indian Civil Service have been made available for Indians, and, but for the War, more might have been heard of the Commission and its Report.

Fisher, who greatly valued his family connections with India, not only shared the old Whig interest in the intelligent administration of our Imperial dependency, but (a rare thing among Englishmen) he showed an appreciative understanding of the great cultures of India, ancient and modern, and he was an enthusiastic student of the writings of Rabindranath Tagore and Toru Dutt. The devotee of Goethe and Dante responded eagerly to the mystics and sages of the East. Service on the Commission gave him a welcome opportunity of seeing India for himself, where he visited, among other places, Lahore, Delhi, Peshawar and Agra, continually fascinated by contrasts of life, colour and landscape, and roused to enthusiasm by the architecture, notably by that of the Deccan. But he was deeply disappointed with the majority of those native officials whom he saw. ' We have had all the most eminent members of the community before us,' he wrote, ' lawyers, judges, journalists, historians, and with two or three exceptions they have not impressed us as rising above mediocrity. And I came out prepared to admire. The Indian Civil Service is terribly unpopular with the Indian intellectuals; indeed, the work of the Service does not bring its members across the new India. Their business is to rule the villagers, whom they mostly love, and by whom they are held in affection and respect.'

In a conversation Fisher afterwards confessed that he thought his service on this Commission had been a waste of time. This was probably due to his belief that the root of the matter lay in education in India, and the Commission's terms of reference barely touched on this. ' We ought to improve the material prospects of the teachers, obliterate the race barrier, raise the matriculation age from 16 to 18, limit the number of students in government colleges, revise the curricula, stock the libraries, and break down the tyranny of examinations.' Social reform could be effective only if accompanied by educational reform. He was destined soon to propose the same solution for problems nearer home.

The outbreak of war in August, 1914, was both a surprise and a disappointment to Fisher: a surprise, because he had not recently been on the Continent, and a disappointment, because though he knew the ambitions of the militant element in Germany, he thought that the strong common sense of the German middle classes would provide sufficient counterbalance to the hysteria of the Emperor and the belligerency of the generals. Also, he thought that the two countries, so closely united in race, in religious sentiment and in the enlightenment of advanced civilisations, would never, except for grave cause, go to war. He believed, in spite of recent crises such as that of Agadir, that there existed in international relations a certain deadweight or inertia sufficient to maintain an equilibrium which seemed part of a moral scheme of things. The tirades of Treitschke and Bernhardi would, he assumed, prove as ephemeral as those of the gutter Press. In these respects he was not unlike most of his educated English contemporaries. He disliked war, and as a Gladstonian he had never 'budgeted' for war. But, with the violation of Belgian neutrality, he knew that Britain must intervene.

A few months after the outbreak of hostilities he asked Sir Edward Grey a question which has been prompted in the minds of many observers by the apparent fact that German calculations had not allowed for the contingency of British intervention on behalf of Belgium. Surely, it was thought, if in earlier years we had made clear our determination to uphold Belgian neutrality in accordance with our obligation, Germany would never have gone to war? Grey's answer was categoric. In the first place he would have had to ask the Cabinet to pledge itself in advance and, as it were, in cold blood to fight for Belgium; he would have had to select one of our many international obligations and secure a commitment that, in a hypothetical set of circumstances, we would fight for that particular commitment. In regard to Germany, the difficulties would have been immensely greater, for at the outset he would have had to insult Germany by indicating what British policy would be in the event of Germany's violating her own obligation to maintain the neutrality of Belgium, and this at a time when he was doing all in his power to improve the relations between the two countries. This unusual kind of situation was to be repeated in later years, and indeed the best justification of Grey is to be found in the events of the years immediately preceding 1939, when those European statesmen who faced the facts hardly dared to suggest what they knew Germany was about to commit, lest they might offend an extremely sensitive national 'honour,' just as a tactful householder, surprised by an armed burglar, might hesitate to make insinuations about the intentions of his unexpected guest. Hence a new difficulty in international relations. In negotiating with the more modern type of national leader it may be impossible to tell in which part he is more sensitive

—in his moral outfit or in his trigger touch. The older diplomacy was neither so thin-skinned nor so quick.

To Sheffield as to other universities the war brought an entirely new set of problems. Many students and members of the staff joined the Forces, though it was not till 1916 that a serious depletion was threatened. Meanwhile, by his eloquent addresses Fisher provided some guidance for a public which, at first, was stunned. He was soon called upon to undertake a more disagreeable form of national service. In September, 1914, he was appointed a member of the Commission, under the chairmanship of Lord Bryce, to investigate alleged German atrocities in Belgium. The members, who included Sir Frederick Pollock, Sir Edward Clarke, Sir Alfred Hopkinson, Mr. Harold Cox and Sir Kenelm Digby, were, for the most part, surprised and shocked to find that so many of the allegations were proved, and to Bryce, a trained jurist and old friend of Germany, the convincing character of the evidence in so many cases brought distress as well as disillusionment. What impressed the Bryce Commission most was that behind the conduct of Germans, notably in Belgium, was a definite, almost scientific system, sponsored by the Government, and clearly enunciated as early as 1902 in the official *Kriegsbrauch im Landskriege*. This was the fact most speedily forgotten by the British public, which, though at first surprised by the revelations of the Report, promptly concluded that, since some of the alleged atrocities had not been proved, therefore all the others had been greatly exaggerated. It was felt by many that, while the findings of the Bryce Commission might have their temporary value as propaganda, they provided no authoritative evidence about German national character, which, it was contended by many Englishmen of education, was in essence as reasonable and moderate as our own. Others argued that any atrocities committed were the work of a small criminal minority, forgetting that even more important than the criminal is the public opinion which condones or approves his acts.

The year 1916 brought Fisher into still closer contact with the conduct of the struggle. In April of that year, on the invitation of the British Government, he went to France in order to study the French system of 'propaganda.' After a visit to the trenches near Rheims he was shown over the Bureau de la Presse in Paris, where he was introduced to several French journalists and publicists. The propaganda department was directed by a Monsieur Bréal, who interested Fisher:

> 'Mons. Bréal expects much from the liberal party in Spain. He gets Spanish men-of-letters to write articles for French newspapers, and these are then translated by Spanish newspapers. He also arranges for photos of fat German prisoners eating big dinners, and the photos are scattered by the thousand over the German lines. He gets letters from Germany to South America intercepted, and substitutes pro-Ally tracts.'

More important even than Monsieur Bréal was Monsieur Adolphe Smith, whose curious name may have been a help in the attempts to dispel French suspicions of English good faith. Monsieur Smith assured Fisher that his was the most difficult work of all. He had already toured the country with the English Mr. Hodge in the hope of convincing the French Labour Party that England was not intent only on making money out of the war. Smith was anxious to arrange another such tour in the South of France, followed by a visit to English industrial cities by two French soldiers—one of them an officer who would be 'extremely revolutionary' in language, the other a *poilu* who would be a 'moderate idealist.' 'These citizens would appear in uniform on British platforms accompanied by Adolphe, who would translate their burning words into appropriate English.' This proposed tour was commended also by the secretary of the French Socialist Party, who undertook to distribute English propaganda 'literature' among his fellow-Socialists. There was agreement in the Bureau that the French worker must be taught something about the English war effort, and there was general regret that the French Socialist paper *L'Humanité* obtained its English news from no other source than the Independent Labour Party. Fisher thought that this might be remedied if we could put up 'some mild Fabian' to act as a corrective to Mr. Ramsay MacDonald.

Fisher was impressed by the absence in France of any appreciation of the extent of the British activities, and by a feeling of distrust, intensified after the battle of Verdun; moreover, he found evidence of actual depreciation of the part which Britain was playing in the war. This was attributed in some quarters to the American colony in Paris, and to the Continental edition of the *Daily Mail*. As a result of his visit Fisher thought that more could be done by personal tours and photographs than by articles in the Press. He was interested to learn that the two of his fellow-countrymen who had the greatest vogue in France were Mr. Lloyd George and Mr. H. G. Wells. He suggested to his old teacher Charles Bémont that he should write for French students a short summary of English History, and he also arranged for greater co-operation in the propaganda conducted by the two countries. Though doubtful about the value of such methods of influencing opinion, and though impressed by the obvious *gaucherie* of some exponents of this art, he did his best to ensure that the weapon would be more effective.

Meanwhile, from his experience as Vice-Chancellor of Sheffield and a former Oxford don, Fisher was disturbed by the serious wastage caused by the war in the ranks of young and highly educated men. Many of these were of exceptional intellectual promise, others were men of great achievement; was it impossible to salvage something from what remained of the talent which the nation could least afford to lose? The country at large was not deeply concerned in this side of the war; the call was for men and more men, and any attempt to distinguish their value for purposes other than cannon fodder would have appeared invidious. But Fisher made an attempt. He drew up a memorandum in which he pointed out the ultimate dangers of sacrificing these young men who were recognised as leaders in intellectual pursuits, and pleaded for some use of their services in a non-combatant capacity. Greatly daring, he sent this to the War Office. The reply was not encouraging. He was advised to confer with other heads of universities—avoiding publicity—in order to select a certain number of 'the brainiest and most efficient fellows upon whom the future of their colleges and universities depends' and also the names of the units in which they were serving. The list 'should not be large.' It might be possible, the reply stated, to transfer some of the chosen few into labour battalions or garrison units, alternatives which would have been repudiated by the men for whom Fisher was making his appeal.

It was at this period, late in the autumn of 1916, that Fisher first attended one of Mr. Lloyd George's famous breakfast-parties, when the subject of peace terms was discussed:

'I suggested that the Allies should be content with the liberation of the occupied French and Belgian territory, with the return of Alsace-Lorraine to France, the cession of Trieste and the Trentino to Italy, and a federal constitution for the Austrian Empire. But Lloyd George, with his belief in small nations, had already made up his mind to the break-up of the Hapsburg Empire, and regarded this as the first step to a democratic organisation of Europe. He spoke of the grievances of the Czechs, the Slovaks, the Roumanians. I thought that their grievances might be met by a wise scheme of federation. Two years later my solution was impossible. The old Empire had crashed to the ground, and insurgent nations were in power. Had peace been made in 1916 a federal Austrian Empire might have survived to police the Danubian region, but after Vittorio Veneto[1] an Austrian Empire of any kind was out of the question.'

Fisher was not alone in thinking that a compromise in 1916 would have proved more durable than the 'definitive' peace of 1919. The breakfast-party had brought into contrast two great exponents of Liberalism—the one in high office, buoyant, dynamic, unrestrained by that sobering form of experience which comes from prolonged study of history; the other still in the academic world, devoted to the cause of justice in the abstract, but imbued with a profound reverence for those ancient institutions and makeshift arrangements which, however imperfectly, had at least succeeded in working. It was as if Rousseau had dined amicably with Burke. This unusual association was soon to be cemented by corporate responsibility, and served at least to enrich the personal element in the political background of the concluding stages of the Great War.

December, 1916, was a period of stock-taking. The costly battle of the Somme was over; the Allies, it is true, had won no great amount of territory, but at least they had forced back the German Army. Should we content ourselves with this achievement? Or should we hold on, until with our more slowly-mobilised reserves we had attained an incontestable superiority? Whatever doubt there may have been about these alternatives, there was little doubt that Mr. Asquith's leadership, though assiduously praised by a small

[1] The name given to the crushing victory of British and Italian forces over the Austrians on October 30, 1918.

body of adherents, was inadequate for the situation, and on the fall of his Ministry Mr. Lloyd George formed a new coalition. He asked the Vice-Chancellor of Sheffield to act as President of the Board of Education in succession to Lord Crewe. Fisher accepted. On December 14 he was sworn-in to his ministerial office; and he was speedily adopted Member of Parliament for the Hallamshire division of Sheffield. His political career had begun.

V

The Education Bill of 1918

FISHER'S acquaintance with school-teaching had never amounted to more than a few weeks spent in undergraduate days in an elementary school; nor did he ever claim to be an educational expert. To this extent he was similar to his predecessors at the Board of Education. But his appointment was a novel one for two reasons—he was brought into the Cabinet without any previous parliamentary experience, and he was the first person of academic or intellectual distinction to be entrusted with this Presidency, an office which in the past had provided an honourable but innocuous resting-place for those statesmen who were not considered suitable for more active or responsible duties. In his construction of the Coalition Ministry of December, 1916, Mr. Lloyd George not only brought in ability from outside, but, in his determination to couple the vigorous prosecution of the war with the initiation of social reform, he included Fisher in the Cabinet, with an undertaking that money would be found for ambitious educational measures. The appointment was popular, both in Parliament and in the educational world. But when Fisher told Mr. A. J. Balfour of his acceptance of the office, the latter raised his eyebrows, and expressed misgiving that a man of ability should go to the Board of Education.

In directing attention during a crisis of the war to the need for vast schemes of social reform Mr. Lloyd George was rightly interpreting the mood of the nation. Great armies, first of volunteers and then of conscripts, were engaged abroad in conflicts of unprecedented magnitude; warfare was being waged with technical equipment for the use of which some scientific knowledge was necessary; many thousands of young men drawn from civil life had to be trained quickly for the responsibilities of command; and the two Services, hitherto small, professional and exclusive, were, for the time being, swamped by youths who had to learn in months what in peace-time had been the work of years, while an entirely new Service, the Air Force, had to be created. The response made by the young to these demands not only confuted the ever-recurrent opinion of the Continent that British democracy is effete, but proved that our national standard of education was at least as good as that of more widely-advertised foreign models. To the surprise of many, it was found that the highly educated are not only better able to master the technique of modern warfare, but that they are capable of an endurance and fortitude hitherto associated mainly with the stupid and the unimaginative. All this helped towards a keener appreciation of the value of education. Another factor was at work. Men were deeply impressed by the tragedy and waste of war. Surely from this sacrifice some great good must emerge? Surely we must close our ears to the cynics who say that war merely breeds war? So, against this background of loss and suffering, endured mainly by the young, the stage was set for educational reform. But the background would not always be the same.

At this point a reference may be permitted to some traditions in the earlier development of education[1] in England, for only in relation to these traditions can the Fisher Act of 1918 be properly understood. The Church was the first educator, and much of mediaeval piety found expression in charities for the education of the young. By the close of the Middle Ages England was well endowed with grammar schools providing a training which, while it included religion, was never 'denominational,' since that term implies the existence of different kinds of faith. Nor is it clear that these schools were obliged to provide for the sons of the very poor, because the *pauperes et indigentes* of mediaeval deeds may have meant not the destitute, but simply those who were not well-to-do. Most of these grammar schools have survived into modern times, either for their original purpose—namely, to provide a good and nearly free education of a secondary or advanced type for children of a district, often an agricultural district, which can maintain a justifiable interest and pride in its school—or, transformed into what are called public schools, these foundations supply an expensive education for boarders who may come from any part of the country.

[1] For a good account see C. Birchenough, *History of Elementary Education in England and Wales.*

Both types of school usually provide facilities for the study of Latin and Greek, and the non-residential type of school met the needs of those parents who are willing and even anxious to pay moderate fees for the education of their sons.

Meanwhile the Industrial Revolution not only intensified the problem of poverty but, by its drastic re-distribution of population, separated many of the old grammar schools from the poorer middle class, for whom they were originally intended, a separation which becomes obvious by comparing industrial areas, where few such schools are to be found, with cathedral cities and county towns, where they mostly survive. Moreover, most of the public schools founded within the last hundred years are located in the countryside, and are carefully dissociated from those local connections which meant so much in the older system; in this way, our expensive boarding schools provide not only for health and for a valuable training in corporate life, but they ensure complete insulation from local dialect, and strive to eradicate what was once a characteristic feature of English life—provincialism, now the monopoly of what are often called the 'lower classes.' The great development of such schools is one of the most striking things in the rapid evolution of our civilisation during the nineteenth century, an evolution in which material and economic expansion was quickly accompanied by social re-adjustment; and it was in the deep ruts of social cleavage so created that our present-day educational system was moulded— for the rich, the public school, famous and distinctive; for the poor, the 'National' or 'Board' school, mass-produced, anonymous and despised. Meanwhile, for the middle classes, unable to afford the public schools, there was this handicap that few of the older grammar schools were available in the districts where they were now most urgently required, namely, in the industrial areas. Education, which might at least have tried to encourage more equal opportunity, followed and emphasised the class distinctions insisted upon not so much by birth or achievement as by money, and in this process the poorer middle class suffered most. This is one of the reasons why Fisher's Act could not provide for a national system at all.

Equal opportunity is denied by nature, but nevertheless, in a planned civilisation, some approach to it can be tried, for example by endeavouring to ensure that, through education, all children, whatever the means of their parents, shall have the chance of entering the learned professions or the higher branches of the Civil Service, as once in Scotland and some other countries. The avenue is the university, and the test is personal aptitude. Now it is still true that for such an education a knowledge of Latin is almost always essential; moreover, Latin has usually to be started in early youth, or never at all. It was once fashionable for successful public men to attribute their success in life to the intellectual and moral advantages of a sound classical education, but one may well conjecture what would have been the difference had these eminent men received their education, not at a public school, or grammar school, where they had to learn Latin, but at a Board school, or secondary school, where they might well have had no chance of doing so. Their boasted advantage was really as much social as intellectual or moral, because, for some reason never clearly explained by educational experts, the poor of England have this among their distinguishing disabilities, that they rarely in childhood have the chance of beginning Latin. This cannot be because of expense, since no elaborate equipment is necessary; nor is it fair to say that many of the poor would fail to profit thereby, for the same can be said of the rich. Whatever be the differences of opinion about the value of a classical education, there can be no doubt that even to-day it provides opportunity, and this is the opportunity which has been studiously withheld from the English poor in even the most elaborate and expensive schemes of educational reform.

But the most subtle of the disguises under which social distinction has reacted on our educational history is the religious disguise, notably in the distinction between Anglican and Nonconformist. The division between these two branches of what used to be called the Protestant faith dates from the Act of Uniformity of 1662, one of the most unfortunate pieces of legislation ever placed on the Statute Book. Excluded from the established church and the two universities by this Act, penalised by the Clarendon Code, and then ostracised by the Test Act, the numerous branches of Protestant dissent became united in their distrust and dislike of the privileged Anglican. They had other things in common, for the Lollards of the fifteenth century, the Independents of the seventeenth, the Wesleyans of the eighteenth and the Congregationalists of the nineteenth century were mostly townsmen—weavers, small merchants, artisans and shopkeepers, between whom and the Anglican squire of the countryside there was a social barrier, preserved intact because, as it could be surmounted, it did not have to be broken down. It was surmounted by making money in the town and buying an estate in the country, with a change-over to Anglicanism. So the distinction remained strong, because it was social, not religious, or even economic; and the new families, as they became accepted in their more privileged surroundings, provided by far the strongest supporters of the barrier, because they had had the trouble and expense of getting over it. Hence the exceptional amenities of our countryside, because these usually have the backing of capital, which cannot so easily be accumulated in the country; hence also the strength of our democracy, which is constantly re-invigorated by this flow of fresh blood into the arteries of even our most exclusive social castes; and so, in the descendants of bourgeois peers and in the heirs of ennobled communists we see the present and future bulwarks of conservatism and conformity. But this has been disastrous for the cause of national education, because the two branches, of what, for want of a better word has to be called Protestantism, always insisted, or were instigated to insist, on separate denominational schools, each of them supplying religious instruction suitable to the doctrinal principles professed, or presumed to be professed, by the parents. In this way the 'consciences' of English parents, as well as proving a heavy burden to the rates and taxes, have been the most serious barrier to educational progress for more than a century, and a foreigner studying our *educational* history might be tempted to assume that there is far more antagonism between Anglican and Nonconformist than between Anglican and Roman Catholic. Such an observer might deduce that this antagonism is more social than theological, and he might insist that it is out of place most of all in the schools, where at least the young should, as far as possible, be spared those dissensions which divide their elders, or are alleged to divide them. In both the drafting and working of his Education Act Fisher tried to avoid this old obstacle, but he did not wholly succeed.

Here again Scotland in the past provided an eloquent contrast.

THE EDUCATION BILL

In that elysium of exegetists religious differences were numerous
and acute, but social distinctions were correspondingly weak, and
so the educational system was enabled to concentrate on the ideals
of cheapness, thoroughness and efficiency, unembarrassed by the
necessity, or even the possibility, of providing the children with
religious instruction suitable to the shade of Protestantism professed
by the parents, many of them keen, amateur theologians, who
insisted that if the schools provided a factual knowledge of the Bible,
together with practice in repeating from memory the questions and
answers in the Shorter Catechism, the home and the kirk would do
the rest. Burgher contested fiercely with Anti-Burgher, families
were divided by Disruption and Secession; United Presbyterians
were united in their suspicions of Established Presbyterians, but
the children went to the same school nevertheless, where the refresh-
ing rain of a liberal educational fell alike on the Free and the Wee
Free.

This dualism of Anglican and Nonconformist is manifest in the
history of voluntary efforts to educate the poor. In 1798 a Quaker
named Joseph Lancaster started a school for poor children in South-
wark, based on two principles—voluntary payment of fees and the
monitorial system, whereby the older pupils taught the younger.
The experiment was so successful that a society, the Royal Lancas-
terian Society, was founded in order to promote the system, and
in 1814 this was reconstituted as the British and Foreign School
Society. Many schools were established under the auspices of this
body, all of them religious, but none denominational; indeed,
Lancaster's main intention had been to teach the poor to read the
Bible, and his schools were attended by children of Anglican and
Nonconformist parents, who do not appear to have been offended
by what was later called 'protoplasmic Christianity.' But the success
of the experiment caused the stricter Churchmen to take alarm, and
in 1811 Joshua Watson, a philanthropist, helped to institute the
National Society for the promotion of schools in which the religious
teaching was to be denominational and Anglican. Both these
pioneers achieved their object. Both shared the fear expressed by
many of their contemporaries that a well-educated poor would be
a national danger, for book-learning was associated with Jacobinism.
Lancaster prepared the way for the Board schools, Watson for the

modern Church schools, and their success, while helping to emphasise the need for early instruction of the poor, served also to deepen
the cleavage between two great sections of English life. Tory,
Churchman and the *Quarterly* on one side of the net, Radical,
Dissenter and the *Edinburgh* on the other, with education as the
shuttlecock tossed from one side to the other—such was the ominous
result of the first serious attempt to deprive the poor of their
illiteracy.

Hitherto, in educational matters, the State had been passive.
Lord Brougham, impressed by the achievements of Lancaster and
Watson, realised the need for State intervention and subsidy, but
his efforts were fruitless, for so long as opinion was divided between
denominational and undenominational teaching there could be no
uniform national system. Both types of school would have to be
subsidised or ignored. So in 1833 a modest beginning was made
when a sum of £20,000 was unobtrusively paid to the two societies
for building schools wherever an equal amount was raised by public
subscription. The grant was increased in 1839, when its distribution
was entrusted to a committee—the Committee of Council on Education; but the subsidy was now available only for those schools where
the Bible was read, and where there was a 'conscience clause'
enabling parents to withdraw their children from religious instruction distasteful to them; there was also provision for inspection of
these State schools. Improvements were effected, as when in 1845
the monitors were abolished and the pupil teachers took their place;
certification of teachers was also introduced, and training colleges
were set up. In 1856 the new office of Vice-President of the Committee of Council on Education was created, and there was needed
only a Gladstonian ministry for the introduction of a sweeping
measure of reform. Already in 1867 the electorate had been greatly
extended by Disraeli's Reform Bill, and all parties were agreed that
voters should have at least the rudiments of education.

To Mr. W. E. Forster, a member of Gladstone's Ministry of
1868–74, is due the first comprehensive measure for the provision of
schools. A Liberal and a Free Trader, Forster was well aware that
no measure could satisfy both Churchman and Nonconformist, and
he knew that already, by the grant initiated in 1833, the State was in
a sense committed to supporting the schools advocated by both

parties. Meanwhile the old animosities were assiduously kept alive by the National Education Union, acting mainly on behalf of the Church of England, and the Birmingham League, favoured by Dissenters and Seculars. Accordingly, Forster decided on a mixture of audacity and compromise. He established a new local authority, the School Board, to be chosen by popular election, the function of which was to provide necessary school accommodation where it was wanting, and to regulate such schools, subject only to the supervision of the Committee of Council. In this way he gave to secular, popularly-elected bodies a control over education, including religious education, in elementary schools subsidised by the State and by the local rates, a measure so daring that in face of strong protest he was obliged to accept an amendment, the famous Cowper-Temple clause which excluded from the Board schools every catechism or formulary distinctive of a creed. This took the denominational or Church schools out of the control of the School Boards, and left these schools dependent on the State grant, which was increased, and on voluntary subscriptions; but the School Boards were empowered to assist the Church schools by a grant from the rates for necessitous children. It was this increased help to the denominational schools which aroused the wrath of the Birmingham League, because (it was held) by this extra subsidy the sectarian schools, whether Anglican or Roman Catholic, Jewish or Nonconformist, would entrench themselves more firmly than ever as obstacles to the ideal of a national education, free, compulsory and secular. The new Board schools, it is true, achieved none of these ideals, though they approximated closely to each; hence the opposition of the League to both parts of Forster's compromise. But, though it had the powerful support of Joseph Chamberlain and John Morley, the League did not quite fit into any of the religious or political divisions of the time, and by trying to do too much, it did nothing at all.

Few measures better illustrate the piece-meal character of English legislation than the Education Act of 1870. It retained the system of fees; it did not make elementary education compulsory; it did nothing for secondary education, and, so far from abolishing the anomalies of the system, it helped to perpetuate them. Moreover, the alignment of forces showed what unexpected difficulties may confront the English educational reformer. Forster, who could not claim to represent any of the rival Churches (he was a Quaker), insisted on the necessity of Bible instruction, and so found himself obliged to defend Christianity against the Birmingham secularists, a defence which would have come more convincingly from the lips of Mr. Gladstone. But Mr. Gladstone was too busy with Ireland, and moreover he regarded the non-sectarian education of the new Board schools as little better than atheism. Such were the dubious auspices under which the scheme was imposed on the tender consciences of the parents. Nevertheless, in their existence of little more than thirty years the School Boards did much for English elementary education. In 1880 they were empowered to enforce attendance in terms of an Act sponsored by Anthony Mundella, then Vice-President of the Committee of the Council, and member for the constituency which Fisher afterwards represented—the Hallamshire division of Sheffield. Mundella, son of an Italian refugee, a Liberal and a member of the Church of England, believed as did Fisher after him that many Churchmen were over-apprehensive of the evils which might result from the teaching of the Bible to children of Anglicans and Nonconformists assembled in the same State-endowed schools.

In many rural districts, where the Boards were captured by the farmers, the State schools were sometimes administered in an unsympathetic and even niggardly way; nor did they always compare favourably with their rural neighbours, the Church schools, where much devoted work was often done by the parson, and by a teaching staff which, though miserably paid, might put into its activities the idealism of a faith. But for large centres of population, in many of which Liberals and Nonconformists predominated, the School Boards provided educational facilities which were the envy of the more precariously-endowed voluntary or Church schools, many of them situated in remote villages, most of them with inadequate premises, and all of them partly dependent on voluntary subscriptions. Hence the School Boards indirectly helped to deepen the old antagonism, and to some it appeared iniquitous that a special rate should have to be paid for the support of Board schools attended by children whose parents, as they did not insist on a sectarian education, were obviously indifferent, and probably immoral. Meanwhile the position of the School Boards was threatened by the Local

Government Act of 1888, which created County Councils and County Borough Councils entrusted, among other things, with the duty of providing technical education. Soon these new local authorities were directing grants for Science and Art teaching to the endowed secondary and grammar schools, and there was an increasing body of opinion, led by the Fabians, against *ad hoc* bodies such as School Boards. With the agricultural difficulties of the 'nineties the voluntary schools found it still more difficult to pay their way, and the demand for equal treatment of the two types of school became so insistent that by 1896 the Conservative Party was pledged to come to the support of the voluntary schools. The School Boards, threatened by a formidable array of Conservatives, Anglicans and Fabians, were suddenly overthrown by a side wind. Unlike the Scottish Boards, the English School Boards had never been empowered to provide for secondary or technical education, but in its day and evening schools the London School Board had given instruction to adults of a non-elementary kind, under the regulations of the Science and Art Department. The Cockerton judgment of 1900, which declared this practice illegal, was the death-knell of the School Boards. They were convicted of having done too much for education. Their duties thenceforth lapsed to the County and County Borough authorities which, as they included the Education rate among numerous other charges, such as Water and Street Lighting, could to some extent divert attention, as the School Boards had been unable to divert it, from the cost of education.

Meanwhile in 1899 the Board of Education was established, and in the more tense atmosphere of the South African War there was, for perhaps the first time, a general feeling that advance in national education is an advance in national efficiency. To meet this demand the Conservative Government carried through the Education Act of 1902, one of the most fiercely contested measures of modern times. On its less controversial side the Act effected a great simplification, for it entrusted to the County and Borough Councils a control, almost complete, over both types of school, and over both secondary and elementary education, so that thenceforth the Board of Education, instead of having to negotiate with 2,568 School Boards and 14,238 bodies of managers, had to deal only with 318 local authorities.[1] The Bill authorised the application of the rates to the support of public secondary schools, and introduced the system of 'free places' whereby a number of poor children from primary schools could, without charge, obtain a secondary or advanced education; but generally speaking the Act, while introducing co-ordination between elementary and secondary school, was mainly permissive in character. The Cowper-Temple type of religious instruction was to be given in the State-provided schools. Otherwise, the Act of 1902 caused opposition, and in some cases repudiation. Many Churchmen and Conservatives were indignant that, by the Kenyon-Slaney clause, the sole control of religious instruction in voluntary schools was taken from the parson and given to the managers of the school, who were now to share their responsibilities with the local authority. But what caused most indignation was that the voluntary or sectarian schools were to be given the benefit of the rates (in addition to the existing Government grant) for repairs to school premises due to fair wear and tear, but not for building or extension. This compromise caused offence on both sides. Advocates of sectarian education complained that Church schools were still left at a serious disadvantage as compared with the provided or non-sectarian schools, which were able to extend and improve their buildings, while their rivals had to carry on with premises often notoriously inadequate. On their side, the Nonconformists objected that, as sectarian education, usually Anglican or Roman Catholic, was now nearly as well endowed as non-sectarian education, the State was in effect subsidising two Churches, one of them uncompromisingly anti-Protestant, while the allegiance of the other to the Protestant faith seemed no better than dubious; indeed, the more devout of the Nonconformists were shocked to see the Scarlet Woman and her demure young sister seated as solidly on the rates as the Police. Answering the criticism that there was no mention of religion in his Bill, Fisher said: 'The friends of religious teaching in our schools should be profoundly grateful that there is no mention of religion in the Bill, and that for once there is a chance of a great measure of educational reform being discussed without any stirring of sectarian passion.'

The Liberal ministries which followed after 1905 made several

[1] L. A. Selby Bigge, *The Board of Education*, p. 17.

attempts to remedy the admitted defects in the Bill of 1902, attempts prompted mainly by a desire to bring the voluntary schools within the control of the local and central authorities. Two Bills, those of 1906 and 1908, provided for the transfer of such schools to the local authority by agreement or compulsion, with facilities for sectarian teaching not at the expense of the rates. Other measures were based mainly on the principle that the voluntary schools might ' contract out,' that is, sever their connection with the rates, and subsist solely on subscriptions and the Government grant. But all these attempts proved abortive, mainly because the parties concerned were unable to agree on terms. This is why, in his Bill of 1918, Fisher preferred to leave the settlement of 1902 undisturbed, and to build on the foundations laid by that Act. But after a few years' experience he had to admit that the old dualism impeded any far-reaching measure of educational reform.[1]

Meanwhile, another aspect of elementary education had come into increasing prominence in the earlier years of the twentieth century—the primary school as a welfare centre, concerned with the physical as well as the intellectual and religious development of the child; and already there existed extensive statutory powers whereby special provision could be made for the defective child, such as the Act of 1893 for the blind and deaf, the Acts of 1899 and 1914 for epileptics, and in general, much of the Public Health legislation was showing more concern for the school and the child. In 1906 the local authorities were empowered to provide cheap and free meals for necessitous children, and in the following year they were authorised to establish vacation schools and play clinics. A School Medical Service as a national institution was established in 1907, mainly for the purpose of administering the Acts of 1893 and 1899, but soon its activities were extended to include the examination and treatment of children, and a dental service was instituted. By 1917 this medical service was a great and highly efficient organisation having a medical staff at headquarters which worked in co-operation with the doctors and nurses appointed by the local authorities, and Fisher had in Sir George Newman an able lieutenant, anxious to implement those clauses in the Bill of 1918 which were intended to safeguard the health and physique of the school child. In drawing up his Bill

[1] See *infra*, p. 80.

Fisher embodied many of the reforms which had for years been demanded by all parties, notably the Liberal and Labour parties, and so his scheme was of far wider import than any previous educational measure. The new President of the Board was a humanitarian as much as an administrator and educationist. 'The War,' he said, ' was my opportunity.'[1]

Starting on the basis of the Act of 1902 he had to recognise the difficulties created by the dual source of educational finance—rates and taxes. Zeal for education was bound to vary in the areas controlled by the local authorities, for in one district low rateable values would be an obvious impediment, while in other more fortunate areas there might be indifference, or even hostility, to increased expenditure on educational objects. An approach to a uniform system could be made only by increasing the contribution made by the State, for which purpose Fisher arranged that the share borne by the Exchequer should always be a minimum of 50 per cent.; but he considered that local interest would be stimulated by a system of percentage grants, whereby enterprising authorities would be encouraged, and poor localities enabled to embark on schemes which could not have been undertaken on the old system. He had at first (in 1917) hoped to secure greater uniformity by consolidating the administrative bodies into larger units, but in face of opposition this plan had to be abandoned, and so the Bill of 1918 reverted to the administrative areas of 1902. This attempt, by means of percentage grants to stimulate local pride in the schools was one of the essential elements in the scheme of 1918, and it led to closer co-operation between the Board of Education and the County and Municipal authorities. Also, by their obligation to submit schemes to the Board, these authorities had to make more careful scrutiny of the educational needs and resources of their districts.

On this basis the Bill of 1918[2] legislated for the child between the ages of 2 and 18, for secondary and technical as well as for elementary education, and was by far the most comprehensive measure yet introduced. Fees in elementary schools were abolished. The age for compulsory education was raised to 14, but this proved very difficult of enforcement. In industrial districts, notably in

[1] *Unfinished Autobiography*, p. 103.
[2] For the text of the Bill see A. A. Thomas, *The Education Bill of 1918*.

Lancashire, there was a system of part-time or even half-time employment of children, and many parents were unable or unwilling to forgo the weekly wages earned by the children; equally the employers were anxious to retain this source of cheap labour. The President worked hard to induce parents and employers to make some sacrifice for the children. ' Every development of public education in this country,' he said in a speech at Manchester, ' has withdrawn juvenile labour from the market, and has at the same time helped to increase the aggregate wealth of the community,' and he added that the physique of the children in factory areas was notoriously poor. His Bill (which ended the ' half-time' system) enacted that children under 12 should not be employed at all, and that those over 12, in attendance at school, should not be employed on Sundays for more than two hours, or on school-days before the close of school hours, or on any day before 6 a.m. or after 8 p.m. The employment of children under 14 in street trading, factories, workshops or mines was forbidden altogether, and the local authorities were empowered to obtain particulars of a child's employment from the parent or employer. But the application of some of these measures had to be postponed, and it may be doubted whether they can ever prove effective. There is continual leakage from evasion. There is the necessity of close co-operation between the local authority on the one hand and, on the other, the Certifying Factory Surgeon, the Labour Exchange and the Juvenile Employment Committee. Moreover, the consequences of excessive labour on the child, as they are not immediately obvious, often escape detection, but they are consequences which lay the foundation for disease. Fisher attached great importance to those parts of the Act which attempted to limit the industrial exploitation of the child, and, though he did not wholly succeed, he at least initiated this important movement of social and educational reform.

For the child over 14 the provisions of the Bill were equally notable. Local authorities were empowered to raise the school-leaving age to 15 and, with the consent of the Board, children might continue to receive instruction in public elementary schools until the age of 16. For those over 14 who showed the requisite degree of intelligence courses of advanced instruction had to be provided. This was usually done in Central Schools, and in this way the old evil of

' marking time' was diminished; but the Bill aimed also at trans-
ference to secondary and technical schools of those elementary
school children who showed signs that they would profit thereby, or
in the more general language of the Act, ' adequate provision shall
be made to secure that children and young persons shall not be
debarred from receiving the benefits of any form of education by
which they may be capable of profiting through inability to pay
fees.' In effect, this clause required the authorities to ensure the
passage of suitable children from elementary to secondary and
technical schools by the provision of scholarships, bursaries, free
places and maintenance grants. What this meant may be deduced
from the fact that in 1917 there were about two million children
in elementary schools considered suitable for higher education who
had no chance of going to secondary schools.[1] In this way much of
the permissive element in the Bill of 1902 was made compulsory.

For children between the ages of 2 and 5 nursery schools had
to be provided, or additions made to those already established. At
the same time the duty of maintaining medical inspection and treatment was extended to all children under 18, whether in elementary
or in secondary schools, and the local authorities were also empowered to prosecute parents for neglect. A further duty imposed
on the authorities was that of finding out what children were
physically defective or epileptic, and of providing for their education
and, where necessary, their maintenance, between the ages of 7 and
16. School camps were also to be set up. It was one of the main
purposes of the Act to encourage the local authorities to prepare
adequate plans on these lines for submission to the Board of
Education, and many of the schemes so submitted show that local
enterprise had been stimulated.

A novelty in the Bill was the clause requiring persons under 18
to attend a day continuation school for not less than 320 hours per
annum. This was new in England,[2] where only voluntary continuation classes in the evening had been instituted, but it was known in
Germany, where it had been started after the Franco-Prussian War,
and it had been tried in several other countries. Fisher regarded this
instruction of ' young persons' as an essential feature of his Bill

[1] B. Yeaxlee, *Working out of the Fisher Act,* p. 18.
[2] For this see E. A. Waterfall, *The Day Continuation School in England.*

because otherwise it seemed to him that there was a great wastage, due to the fact that, even in his scheme, the education of the child ceased at 14, when development was becoming most rapid. The result was often a complete sacrifice of what the child had already learned, and so the compulsory day continuation school was proposed as an alternative to the voluntary secondary and technical school. This was destined to prove one of the most controversial things in the Bill, and indeed it never came into general effect, though it was tried by a few authorities such as London, Stratford-upon-Avon and Swindon, and in several places, notably Rugby,[1] it has proved a great success. The project—for in the end it amounted to no more than a project—raised in an acute form the old controversy between general and vocational education, and it is of interest that, while many working-class parents favoured the latter, the Labour Party on the whole was in favour of a general education which at least would open up wider opportunities for the child. Here again the Bill of 1918 had little permanent effect, but it provided a precedent which has revived in recent years.

The Fisher Act rested on three supports of which two have been mentioned, namely, an increased grant from the Exchequer and special financial encouragement of those local authorities which, whatever their resources, showed enterprise for the cause of education. The third support was the teacher. Fisher was the first President of the Board who showed sincerity in his contention that our educational system was suffering seriously from the poor status and the inadequate salary of the school-teacher, and at the outset he made it clear that he wished to effect an improvement. Knowing the indifference of many local authorities on this point, he arranged that three-fifths of the cost of salaries should be contributed by the State, and he set up a committee under the chairmanship of Lord Burnham to formulate a standard minimum scale for secondary and elementary teachers. The immediate change was drastic. In 1913–4 the average salary of elementary school teachers was £99; in 1919 it was £184. It was made clear by both Fisher and Lord Burnham that this increase must be regarded not as a war-time bonus, to be taken away as soon as the cost of living appeared to be diminish-

[1] The continuation school there is the only survivor of those which came into existence under the Act of 1918.

ing, but as a belated reform, intended to inaugurate a clearer recognition of the value to the State of the teachers' services. He also, in 1917, initiated for teachers a contributory pension scheme, but the application of this some years later caused considerable dissatisfaction, because the enforced contribution had to be made at a time when the salaries were being subjected to reductions.

Long before the introduction of the revised Bill to the House of Commons on January 14, 1918, Fisher had won the respect of the House by his quick adaptation to parliamentary traditions, and by the high seriousness of his speeches. At the Second Reading on March 13 there was a note of opposition[1] on the ground that Parliament, then in its eighth year, was not really representative and had no mandate for educational reform. Objection was also taken to the phrase 'national system of education available for all persons capable of profiting thereby.' How could a scheme be called national when it left out the rich? Did 'profiting' mean the profitable use of an education in the sense of using it for the purposes of a career? A more concrete criticism was that the part-time education of all children up to the age of 18 would cause serious dislocation in agriculture and industry, and would be prejudicial to those youths who were not likely to benefit by instruction beyond the age of 14. 'You will make prigs of the young persons, not tradesmen or housewives.'[2] Some complained that, by extending compulsion, the Bill was an advance towards the Socialist doctrine that the child is no more than a unit in the State, of value mainly as a potential breeder; others objected to the increased powers assumed by the Board of Education, whereby it appeared to constitute itself a judge in its own cause, and Fisher the Liberal must have experienced a shock when he was publicly accused of 'setting up a latter-day Star Chamber in respect of young persons, as he calls them.' Moreover, the proposed day continuation schools came in for some criticism, mainly on the ground that they would interfere with the apprenticeship system, and there was also some Roman Catholic objection to the Bill, apparently on the ground that its spirit was secular, and from apprehension that the powers of the managers of Roman Catholic schools would be diminished. Fisher was able to allay anxiety on this score.

[1] *Hansard*, CIV, 335 *ff.*   [2] *Ibid.*, p. 353.

While gratified by the enthusiastic reception given to the Bill by Liberal members the President was disappointed with the response of the Labour Party. Some Labour members scented bureaucracy; others wanted a more sweeping, national measure; others were against all forms of vocational training, and some even suspected a military element in the school camps. It is possible that at this time the Labour Party was not agreed on educational policy, owing perhaps to multiplicity of counsellors, all united on the principle of 'equal opportunity for all,' but differing on the practical measures for putting this maxim into practice. This may have been in the mind of Sir F. Banbury, then the most forcible exponent in the Commons of an old-fashioned Toryism. He disliked the Bill because it was revolutionary, and, 'as far as my experience goes revolutions generally are bad.' 'Does education give you the ablest race of men?' he asked, and supplied the answer by recounting his unfavourable experience of Oxford graduates in the City. Also, he disliked the phrase 'Appointed Day,' the day to be decreed by the Board for bringing into effect the various provisions of the Bill; possibly it appeared that a Government department was arrogating for its edicts an expression hitherto reserved for the decrees of Providence. 'How,' asked Sir F. Banbury, 'is education going to assist a man who has to spread manure on a field?'[1] Fisher did not attempt to answer that question.

At intervals in the summer of 1918 the Bill was discussed in committee. A proposal to make the continuation schools voluntary was negatived by 106 to 29; equal payment for the sexes was proposed on July 15 and lost by 93 to 25. These figures suggest that the debates were not very well attended. At the third reading it was objected that the Bill vested too much power in the Board of Education which, by its encouragement of ambitious schemes proposed by the local authorities, would thereby cause both diversity and extravagance. More was to be heard of this objection within a few years. Nevertheless the Bill passed the Commons on July 16, and after being successfully negotiated through the lords by Lord Lytton became law on August 8. In 1921 it was embodied in a consolidated measure which, with a few amendments, remained the statutory code of our educational system until 1944, but effect was given only to a small propor-

---

[1] *Ibid.*, pp. 429-432.

tion of its reforms, and the great economy drive of 1920–2 caused an indefinite postponement of most of the schemes on which Fisher had set his heart.

But even before the Geddes Axe fell on the necks of the Government departments, difficulty was experienced in the working of the Bill, owing mainly to shortage of teachers and to the greatly increased cost of building. In March, 1920, Fisher startled the educational world by proposals designed to modify not only the Bill of 1918 but also the settlement of 1902.[1] He put forward a scheme intended to ensure for the local authorities full control over the appointment and dismissal of teachers (hitherto shared with the managers of voluntary schools); that no teacher should be required to give religious instruction unless specially appointed for that purpose; that the local authorities should have free use of the premises of voluntary schools in return for defraying all the costs of their upkeep, and that the local authorities should provide in all elementary schools for religious observance and instruction, differentiated as far as possible in relation to religious tenets, to be given in school hours by teachers willing to give it, subject to a conscience clause. A Bill on these lines was introduced, but was not proceeded with.

These proposals show how far Fisher was prepared to go in order to end a state of matters which he believed to be prejudicial to even the best-planned schemes of educational reform. For the sake of uniformity, and in order both to have the use of much-needed school buildings and to come to the help of the Church schools, he was prepared to introduce into all the elementary schools sectarian instruction, with only the safeguard of a conscience clause. Nothing could better illustrate the strength of that tradition in English education which imposed on the school the duty of providing denominational teaching; and the increasing demand for such instruction must, to the external observer at least, appear a melancholy indication of the declining influence of both the home and the Protestant churches. Moreover an important principle was at stake. Once it is admitted that the State must provide for every variety of doctrine professed or alleged to be professed by the parents,

[1] For this see L. A. Selby Bigge, *The Board of Education*, pp. 227 ff., and *The Times*, March 29, 1920. For Lord Sheffield's criticism of the proposal see *The Times*, April 7.

then this objection is bound to be made that, while we are willing to make sacrifice in order to encourage the teaching in schools of religious doctrines which we know to be good, we must endure the mortification of seeing our sacrifice frustrated by enforced contribution to the propagation in other schools of opinions which we know to be bad.[1] Nor is this all. It would be a disaster if the imperishable literature of the Bible ceased to be read in our schools, but on the other hand is it fair to impose on the naturally honest minds of the young those subtleties about doctrine which have been evolved by their expert elders,[2] particularly as there is so much difference of opinion among these experts? From an outside point of view it must appear strange that the elementary school should be chosen as the battle-ground for such interminable squabbles.

Less controversial were the measures adopted by Fisher for enabling demobilised officers and men to pursue courses of higher education at the universities and technical colleges. The cost of the scheme, ultimately about £8,000,000, was at first based on an average cost of about £400 for each of 15,000 men, and the benefits were later extended to Scotland and Ireland. In order to ensure the success of the experiment, the educational institutions concerned were unsparing in their efforts to provide adequate instruction, and in many cases accommodation, for the ex-Service men who brought to their studies a keenness and sense of responsibility rarely found in undergraduates. These students, many of whom could not have obtained advanced education without a grant, helped to dispel the fear that demobilised men, after the uncertainties and dangers of war, would be unable to settle down to routine and regular study; on the contrary some of them proved to be the best pupils within the experience

[1] Cf. the words of Dr. A. C. Headlam, late Bishop of Gloucester, in a letter to *The Times*, November 2, 1943: ' At the beginning of the century many Nonconformists refused to pay rates because they might be used to support Church schools. Churchmen and Roman Catholics pay rates and taxes which are used for the support of schools in which the religious teaching is in their opinion erroneous or inadequate. And yet in addition have to pay large sums for the schools they desire. Is this justice or equality? '

[2] Speaking at a conference of the Educational Association Mr. H. G. A. Gaunt, headmaster of Malvern College, was reported by *The Times* (January 1, 1946) as stating that the creeds are ' unsuitable for our present-day purposes in several ways.' Many of the phrases are merely ' pictorial,' ' but by *ordinary people*, and especially by *young people*, they are taken at their face value, and are therefore gravely misleading.' The conclusion would seem to follow that religious education, as it is now understood, can be safely given only *to* trained experts.

of their teachers, many of whom, it should be recalled, were themselves fresh from the battle-fronts, suddenly called upon to undertake an unusually heavy burden of teaching. The success of this experiment, together with a realisation of the part which the universities and technical colleges might play in war, created an atmosphere favourable to an increased grant to the universities, and for the first time, mainly on Fisher's initiative, the Universities of Oxford and Cambridge received a grant from the Exchequer. It is an interesting fact that the grant to the universities is one of the few items of State expenditure which has survived unscathed from successive agitations for economy; more important, and here the influence of Fisher counted for much, acceptance of the grant has never yet entailed any sacrifice of intellectual independence, as it has so often done on the continent. This is one of the few surviving relics of Gladstonian Liberalism.

But the cause of elementary and secondary education was not so fortunate. Fisher's Bill required for its application a steadily increasing expenditure, falling partly on the rates, but mainly on the State, and it was soon obvious that education is one of the most expensive of the social services. Thus in 1918-9 the Treasury grant for this purpose was about 19 millions; in the following year it was 32 millions, and for 1920-1 the estimate was 43 millions. Concurrently, there was an increasing burden on the rates which provided, on an average, about two-thirds of the amount contributed by the Exchequer. Now that hostilities were over the cry for economy was soon raised, and as early as October, 1919, Fisher was singled out by the *Daily Mail* as one of the 'spending' ministers, and in the House of Commons he was described as one of our most expensive statesmen. The public was given little opportunity of understanding why the education estimates showed such striking increases in the years immediately after the War. This was due not so much to the enforcement of those clauses in the Bill that could be applied at once as to the serious monetary inflation. Most of the increase was in the salaries of teachers, and much of this really measured the extent to which they had been underpaid in the past. Also, with demobilisation, there were more teachers available for the smaller classes which it was the policy of the Board to encourage; building costs were much higher; there were more nursery schools, and the greatly increased demands on the School Medical Service necessitated more expenditure. The country had demanded a large measure of social and educational reform and had got it. But before long it was contended that only those clauses of the Bill should be applied which did not involve extra cost, and in this way many of the essential things in Fisher's scheme were blasted by the icy winds of economy.

On the recommendations of the committee under the chairmanship of Sir Eric Geddes, drastic reductions were effected in every branch of the administration. A total saving of about 8 million pounds in the cost of elementary education was aimed at, to be achieved by raising the lower age limit, increasing the size of classes and reducing the salaries of teachers. A twenty per cent. reduction of staff, or a twenty per cent. reduction of salaries, or a ten per cent. reduction in both, these were the alternatives considered. There was also objection by the Committee to the system of percentage grants, on the ground that, in Scotland at least, the system had encouraged extravagance. It was recognised that there was a strong feeling in the country not only against the cost of education, but against education itself, and there was even a hint that the political parties had allowed the Bill of 1918 to be passed simply as a wartime expedient, which could be quietly dropped when peace returned. Thus, in his last year of ministerial office Fisher was continually on the defensive, anxious to save as much as possible of his scheme, and concerned most of all lest the teachers should suffer.

In his evidence before the Geddes Committee Lord Burnham stated that in the year 1919 the teaching profession was in a state of great unrest. There was a serious shortage of teachers, especially men, and the poorer local authorities could afford only the less efficient teachers, willing to accept a poor salary. In these circumstances the Burnham Committee had carefully considered the salaries of elementary, secondary and technical teachers, for each of which categories a standard minimum scale had been drawn up. For women the scale was four-fifths of that paid to men. The increase of pay on the Burnham scales was not due to war conditions, but to the conviction that for long the teachers had been underpaid. The scales were not meant to be re-adjusted in accordance with alleged changes in the cost of living, but on the other hand Lord Burnham thought that if the rates had been settled in 1922 they would have been somewhat less than those arrived at in 1919-20, when prices were exceptional.

Fisher believed that the secondary teachers would be more willing than the elementary teachers to consent to a temporary reduction, and though he was anxious to avert this sacrifice from both classes of teacher, he was appalled by the alternative, namely, the dismissal of over 40,000 teachers. He was more ready to surrender the education of children under 6 since that pertained to social rather than to educational reform, and he had already been obliged to acquiesce in the postponement of his plan to ensure full-time education of all children under 14, and part-time education of all under 18. Mr. Lloyd George was in favour of securing economy by having classes of sixty to seventy pupils, but Fisher opposed this, preferring a moderate reduction of salaries to wholesale reduction of staffs. In February, 1922, the Prime Minister received a deputation of teachers to which he pointed out that the charge on the Exchequer for education had increased from 14 millions in 1913-4 to 50 millions in 1921-2. The Government, he said, proposed to effect necessary economies by excluding children under 6, closing small schools, increasing the size of classes, and placing the teachers' pensions on a contributory instead of a non-contributory basis (as Fisher had advocated in 1917). The Premier made a strong appeal for the consent of the teachers to the suspension of their increments under the Burnham Scale during the period of financial stringency, which he thought would last no more than a few years. There were, he added, two millions of unemployed who were costing the country one hundred millions a year.

To this appeal the secondary teachers, on the whole, responded readily, but there was considerable heart-burning among the elementary school teachers, many of whom felt that Fisher had betrayed their cause. It is true that, but for the stand made by the President of the Board, the sacrifice demanded of the teachers might have been even greater; nevertheless the fact remains that Fisher to some extent forfeited the extraordinary reputation which he had created in the educational world. It might have been better for that reputation if he had resigned in 1921, or even earlier; but the teaching profession would have fared no better with his successor. Later reductions of pay, such as occurred during the financial crisis of 1931, served still further to embitter the more poorly-paid teachers, who may have been tempted to contrast the glowing eulogies of their profession, poured forth by educational experts not engaged in teaching, with the very modest rewards accorded to the humbler members of that profession. The teachers may have failed to discern a peculiar and unavowed attitude to this question of emoluments. If it is constantly proclaimed that teaching is a noble vocation, to be undertaken only by those who have a natural love for it, then the teachers must not be surprised that hard-headed managers and economical public bodies put the teacher into the same category as the organist and the librarian who, as they are reputed to do their work mainly for the love of it, can accept that pleasurable emotion as part payment of salary. Other professions do not have so many or such eloquent enthusiasts, publicly emphasising the dignity, the privilege and the idealism of their vocations, and so the sordid fact may be overlooked that after all school-teaching is a means of earning a living, and should be provided with the material requisites for maintaining that social status which all are agreed should be a high one.

In general, it is difficult to assess the permanent results of parliamentary legislation, for so many developments in our national life take place outside the scope of legislative enactment, or even in spite of it; moreover, whatever may be true of the present, England in the past was intolerant of codes. One obvious effect of the Fisher Act may nevertheless be indicated—it greatly strengthened and developed our secondary schools, with the result that a much larger proportion of children of poor parents are now able to enjoy an education far in advance of the primary stage. The social and national importance of this is incalculable. On the one hand it has enabled the great professions and industries to recruit their responsible personnel from a much wider field, and has made entry into the higher and middle branches of the Civil Service more selective; on the other hand, this great increase in the proportion of the comparatively well-educated has served us nobly in the war of 1939-45, not only by providing large numbers of young men and women who could quickly be trained for executive posts, but also, more indirectly, by creating a solid core of intelligent and well-informed public opinion, such as can be found nowhere else in Europe. Britain has emerged from that war with responsibilities that would have appalled earlier generations, accustomed to selection of their leaders from a narrower and more privileged minority; but now, however menacing the future may seem, we have the knowledge that the strain, whether of international emergency or of social readjustment, will fall on a population better enabled, mainly by education, to bear it. More than ever before, a sense of tradition and continuity is essential for the proper maintenance of our national life, and our secondary schools have immeasurably extended the basis on which that sense of continuity is imposed.

The Bill of 1918 also focused public attention on the possibilities of State education in this country, and opened up new vistas of what legislation may achieve. Here its influence is more difficult to assess; a least, it is more controversial. There is now a danger that we may demand too much from the School and State, that we may insist overmuch on more legislation and more money, sacrificing the individuality of the school and the personality of the teacher to soulless 'machinery' and cast-iron regimentation; or we may overlook those deep-seated defects in our social system which threaten to nullify the most expensive and elaborate schemes of reform. It is true that we cannot have too much education, but of book-learning we can easily have more than enough. Thus, a boy may be diverted from a highly-skilled craft into a black-coat profession, less by the desire for better emoluments than by his instinctive knowledge of the social disparagement which is still unjustly attached (however much it may be denied) to the manual worker; and the same is even more true of domestic service. It is everywhere admitted that training for a skilled craft, including housecraft, is in itself an education, but can we blame the potentially good workman who elects for a training, at State expense, which will qualify him to be a publicist or agitator because of the superior social status assigned to these occupations? Or the girl, actually a good cook, who receives from the nation an education which will enable her to become an indifferent secretary or a redundant typist? And can the schools replace the homes, broken up by divorce, or the churches, all of them so anxious that their distinctive tenets shall be taught, at public cost, in the schools? Moreover, while we retain our most expensive public and preparatory schools, we insist, by the abolition of fees in other schools, on the elimination of those parents of moderate means who desire to make some sacrifice on behalf of their children, an elimination which, among other serious social consequences, may ultimately help to emphasise the contrast between the rich and poor.

This contrast includes a curious social distinction. The rich demand that the education for which they pay shall be such as will enable their children to enter one of the services or professions, or will qualify them to play their part in public life, and accordingly the money so spent is not unlike a family investment. But for the poor much higher ideals than these are to be fulfilled. Their education by the state is for no materialist object, but to enable them adequately to wield 'the tremendous power which has come into our hands through the processes of democracy':

'The aim of education as I see it is to create a society such as has never existed before, in which men and women are free, independent and responsible, not to themselves, but to each other. It is the purpose of education not to create better human beings, but to create the conditions in which human beings can better themselves mentally, physically and spiritually.'[1]

If this means anything, it may mean that the purpose of state education is not to better the individual, but to create the external conditions in which a utopia will be possible. But is there any consensus of opinion about how such ideal conditons can be achieved? Otherwise, the State school, as thus envisaged, becomes merely a vehicle of political or economic propaganda, rather than a means of training the young for the contest of life.

Fisher made a contribution of permanent importance to the cause of educational reform, and the value of that contribution is not diminished by the fact that so many of its consequences have been obscured, even overlooked by later developments. In these days of administrative revolution and high-pressure publicity, reputation, quickly acquired, may be as speedily and easily forgotten.

'By dint of unwearying patience [wrote The Times] and immense resourcefulness in negotiation, he produced a policy which provided for the complete recasting of the educational

[1] From a speech by Mr. R. Law, Minister of Education, quoted in The Times, June 9, 1945.

system, and yet at once commanded the widest measure of
approval from Parliament and Public. Circumstances favoured
him, it is true. There was a general, keen desire for large-scale
educational advance. Nevertheless, the unhappy history of educational legislation in this country served to throw into bold relief
the greatness of his achievement. Undaunted by the fact that
almost every Education Bill in this country for the past hundred
years or more had been frustrated by denominational controversy
or strife over the instruments of local administration, he boldly
tackled both problems, and wove settlements of each into the
greatest measure of educational reform the country has ever
known.'[1]

These words refer not to the Act of 1918, but to Mr. Butler's Act
of 1944. Had the subject of this biography survived to read them
he might have recalled how Mr. A. J. Balfour had raised his eyebrows into question-marks when Fisher told him that he was going
to the Board of Education.

[1] *The Times*, April 8, 1944.

VI

Cabinet Minister : The League of Nations
1916–22

FISHER had been added to the Cabinet for the express purpose of promoting educational reform, and was not at first consulted on questions of policy outside his department. But in many matters connected with the war and its aftermath his views came to be sought for, and these often had influence with the Prime Minister, between whom and the President of the Board there quickly developed a warm friendship, based on the appreciation by each of similar as well as dissimilar qualities in the other. The Premier found in Fisher a mine of information about Europe and foreign affairs; he liked his subordinate's idealism, his integrity, his enthusiasm for great causes, and at times he was soothed by the equanimity and detachment which his colleague brought to Westminster. This was the more notable as Mr. Lloyd George was not always happiest with those of his colleagues who could boast academic honours; at times, indeed, it seemed that he would have been more comfortable had these been opponents rather than allies. With Asquith and Grey he had to outward appearance worked harmoniously, but the former was usually most at his ease when surrounded by members of his own Oxford college, while the latter sometimes caused resentment by his sustained reticence and austerity. And now in the Coalition there was A. J. Balfour, enigmatic and elusive, occasionally exercising a waspish wit which obliged the victim to search for the place where the sting would be felt; in contrast, there was Lord Curzon, about whom there was no delayed action, a man of great strength of character, but forthright, arrogant and indiscreet. The Prime Minister, somewhat shy of these brilliant products of Balliol and Cambridge, took to his heart Fisher, the humane humanist. On his side Fisher admired the qualities of vision, of indomitable courage, of titanic force, which made Lloyd George our greatest national leader since the days of the elder Pitt.

Fisher's private diary reveals some of the momentous problems which from day to day were considered by the War Cabinet in the concluding stages of the Great War. Throughout the year 1917 the submarine menace was the most serious of all, and the one least likely to be appreciated by the general public, which ever since 1915 was repeatedly assured by experts that the menace had been overcome, whereas there was going on a grim race between measure and counter measure, and at the Admiralty Fisher's younger brother was doing much not, as was commonly supposed, to end the threat of submarine activity, but to gain a move in the struggle which in war-time must be faced so long as surface ships are sinkable. By the end of 1917 our counter-measures had achieved the all-important one move ahead, but the Government decided not to publish the figures showing an improved position lest these might encourage the public to indulge in extravagance in food. In December of that year the feeling in the Cabinet was that the most difficult corner of the war had been turned, but that victory, considered impossible of achievement by the end of 1918, could be attained only when the full weight of American armaments had been put into the field. The solitary statesman who dissented was General Smuts. He thought that the collapse of Germany was near at hand. He made no secret of his opinion that Japan was the enemy of the future. In this gift of intelligent anticipation Smuts was rivalled only by Winston Churchill.

In February, 1918, the President of the Board visited Headquarters Staff in France, where he found Haig both discontented and pessimistic. The Field Marshal did not conceal his opinion of politicians, particularly French politicians, but he expressed a high regard for Pétain. He was deeply disappointed that the importance of the Somme victory had been minimised in England; he was against a continuation of hostilities merely for the recovery of Alsace-Lorraine, and he condemned the Salonica enterprise. Fisher was perturbed by the scepticism shown by Haig and British Headquarters generally about the continuation of the war, now that Russia was out of it, and he noted the low opinion entertained by high British officers both about the amount of the American war contribution and the capacity of American soldiers, many of whom were thought to be amateurs. This traditional contempt felt and expressed by the professional for the amateur, strongest of all in the Navy, had at times threatened to impede the Allied conduct of the war, and here Fisher and Lloyd George were at one. They had an ally in Winston Churchill, all three anxious to ensure that, in the British Army at least, the higher ranks would be open to volunteers who had proved their capacity in the field. But Lord Derby, the secretary of state for War, could do little to promote this policy; indeed, he confessed that he experienced a shock of fear every time he saw a general.

The earlier months of 1918 were among the most anxious of the war. Hopes that large American armies would soon be in the field were not fulfilled; the man-power problem became still more critical, and the War Cabinet considered the question of applying conscription to Ireland. The position at that time was little better than that of two years before when the Easter Rebellion had shown that the older leaders were being displaced by a younger and more violent generation, and a commentary on the situation in the spring of 1918 is supplied by Lord French's expressed belief that British forces in Ireland were sufficient to maintain order and enforce conscription provided permission were given to use aeroplanes. It must now have been evident that the bribe of Home Rule—hitherto kept in reserve for bargaining purposes—was no longer sufficient, and this may be why Fisher refused the Irish Secretaryship in April, 1918. He informed his colleagues that he would be unwilling to enforce conscription, since even the attempt to do so would fail. He was right. This proved one of the few matters on which Fisher disagreed with his chief. On April 29 Lloyd George said that English opinion would applaud the enforcement of conscription on Ireland. No, said Fisher, it would be revolted.

Late in September of this year the President of the Board paid his first visit to Ireland, mainly in order to see for himself the conditions in Irish schools. He recorded his impressions in the following letter to the Prime Minister:

'Indifference to the war is associated with a general ignorance of contemporary events, and with an active hatred of England, and a contempt for English government. The schools in Nationalist Ireland seem to me to be turning out young people unfriendly to England and the English connection. The teachers are underpaid, and are completely controlled by the priestly managers who appoint them; they are for the most part Sinn Fein in their opinions.

'In the agitation against conscription the priesthood has taken a prominent part. The very moment it was known that conscription was to be applied to Ireland, the Principal of Maynooth dismissed all his students to their homes, partly as a protest and partly to increase the difficulty of rounding them up. It was indeed the firm belief of the priests that England was defeated, and that a German army would shortly land on the shores of Ireland. And seeing that the Principal of Maynooth received his education at Freiburg, where he learnt English History from a German professor, it was probable that he was at no special pains to represent this prospect in a repulsive light.

'It is difficult to say how far Nationalist Ireland was, or is, actively pro-German. John Dillon, with whom I had some conversation, holds that German propaganda has gone very far, that a great deal of German money has been spent in the country, and that the sympathies of the major part of the nation are with Germany.... An American journalist, fresh from a visit to County Cork, told me that he found in that county general indignation against the American Republic for having interfered to save the English just when they were satisfactorily beat. It is to be expected that this acute state of disloyalty will, in due course, be abated by the victories of the Allied arms. A general election now would result in a sweeping Sinn Fein victory. A few months hence, assuming a continuance of Allied successes in the war, the result would be otherwise.

'The conduct of the hierarchy has been so directly calculated to injure the prospects of Home Rule that a reasonable doubt has been generated whether the bishops are really in favour of the passage of a Home Rule Bill. Again and again, when prospects seemed fair, the hierarchy has advanced a demand which made settlement impossible. I believe, however, that we should be wrong in thinking that the Irish bishops are opposed to Home Rule. They belong to the peasant class; they have been educated at Maynooth. All through their lives they have been brought up in a Home Rule atmosphere, and seeing that both in public and private they asseverate their loyalty to the Home Rule idea, they would be the most consummate liars in the world if they were in reality opposed to a policy which they so consistently commend to their flocks. The clue to their action lies not in opposition to Home Rule but in a determination to maintain their hold over the political sympathies of the people. They take the action which they think will be popular.

'My view is that the Government should either carry out conscription according to the time-table and give an unmistakable pledge of its plan to proceed with a plan of Irish self-government, or that it should postpone both sides of its policy. On the whole, I have come to the conclusion that the second of these is preferable. . . . It has entered very deeply into the soul of the country that there is a general belief that the Government does not mean business in the matter of Home Rule, that it has deliberately introduced conscription in order to provoke resistance, and that it desires to provoke resistance in order to have an excuse for shelving Home Rule altogether.'

Fisher, in common with most of his English contemporaries, believed that, if rightly handled, Irish opinion would return to more normal courses.

Meanwhile the Germans had launched what was to prove their last great offensive in the war, and as the spring of 1918 changed into summer it seemed that military victory was at last within the enemy's grasp. On June 12, at breakfast, Mr. Lloyd George warned his colleagues to be prepared for the fall of Paris, but he added that Clemenceau would hold out to the end. The situation was saved by measures which revealed the genius of Foch and the tenacity of Haig, and thereafter it seemed to many that at least the old stalemate on the Western Front had been restored; indeed, as late as October, 1918, the Chief of Staff, Sir Henry Wilson, told the War Cabinet that there was nothing in the military situation in France or Belgium which would make a German surrender intelligible.[1] But the internal crisis in Central Europe was now exercising a decisive influence. In November Mr. Churchill, who was then Minister of Munitions, raised the question whether a Ministry of Supply should be created out of the Ministry of Munitions when the war was over, in order to provide and maintain equipment for an army of fifty divisions. It was decided to do this, but the proposal was not energetically pursued, and was ultimately dropped. Meanwhile a scheme

[1] See D. Lloyd George, *War Memoirs*, pp. 3149–50.

of demobilisation was adopted, and the Liberal ministers of the
Coalition proceeded to discuss election prospects. The Prime
Minister thought that Asquith would be too proud to join in a
new Coalition. In order to preserve the political truce it would, he
suggested, be necessary to give the Tories something—for instance,
if they accepted Home Rule, the Liberals in return might give them
some anti-dumping legislation. His subordinates courteously
pointed out that the Premier's best bargaining counter was himself,
since the Tories had no leader to take his place. A few days after this
conversation the nation learned that the Armistice had been signed,
and the Great War ended in a manner which provided the enemy
with some pretext for the contention that his armies had never been
defeated in the field. Nor was this view limited to the Germans.
Five years later, at a luncheon-party, Mr. Lloyd George, alluding to
the 'folly' of the Germans in asking for an armistice, expressed
the opinion that they should have retreated from Alsace-Lorraine
and Belgium, 'and then no Allied army would have fought for
another week against them.'

Even at this time the problem ' what to do with Germany ' was
no new one. Already in his Fourteen Points President Wilson had
enunciated for a Europe of which he knew little, principles, all of
them seemingly innocuous or incontrovertible, but concealing
dangerous possibilities when applied to the facts of inter-state relations. These, at first repudiated by the Germans, were now eagerly
acclaimed by them when defeat was certain; and even before the
Armistice the War Cabinet had to deal with one of the 'Points,'
namely, Freedom of the Seas, the application of which would have
necessitated a surrender by Great Britain of most of the advantages
which, in war, she derived from maritime supremacy. In this matter
the Prime Minister had to be firm with Colonel House, President
Wilson's representative, even to the extent of announcing that, if
necessary, the British Commonwealth would continue to fight alone.
This was an unfavourable augury for the coming peace negotiations,
where much was to be heard of another 'Point,' specially popular
in Ireland, the right of ' self-determination.' But the Fourteen
Points were only one of several panaceas offered to a war-wracked
world at this time.

In November, 1918, Fisher's duties were greatly increased by his appointment to the chairmanship of the Home Affairs Committee, a post which entailed constant attention to the many problems raised by the transition from war to peace. Demobilisation, licensing restrictions, adjustment of subsidies for raw materials, the gradual withdrawal of controls and restrictions, such were a few of the problems on which he had to exercise much thought. He was an ideal chairman. He presented to his colleagues the salient facts of the matter in question with an impartiality comparable with that of a judge; he listened patiently to what was said, bringing the stragglers back to the point, and at the psychological moment, before which a decision would have been premature, and beyond which discussion might be irrelevant or dangerous, he would put the question and obtain a decision. Always imperturbable and impersonal, he was efficient and alert in his handling of men; indeed, his diplomatic skill was one of the assets of the Coalition Cabinet, and at this time his reputation was at its height. In December, 1918, he was urged by Mr. Balfour to accept the office of assistant secretary of state for Foreign Affairs, then about to be vacated by Lord Robert Cecil, but he declined, possibly on the ground that the office was not a full secretaryship of state, or possibly because he felt that he was committed to the cause of education.

The 'Coupon Election' of December, 1918, imposed electioneering duties on Cabinet Ministers, and in the provinces Fisher was impressed by the strong anti-German feeling of the populace, which was sharply contrasted with the more conciliatory tone prevalent among the majority of the educated classes, many of whom, in their own phrase, were anxious 'to put Germany on her feet.' The workers, as a whole, did not share this solicitude for the ex-enemy, though it can be found in the utterances of many of their political leaders. Popular feeling had been buoyed up by the assurances that Germany would be obliged to pay for the whole cost of the war, and that the ex-Kaiser, with other war criminals, would be tried and punished. Of these repeated assurances Fisher was reminded during his electioneering campaign; at Manchester he was met with the additional demand that rents should be regulated, and aliens expelled; while at Crewe he found everyone, especially the mothers, very violent against Germany. 'I am afraid it will take a long time before the feeling dies down,' he noted. He had lost two brothers in the war, but he felt no resentment whatever, and was anxious only that Germany should again take her place in the comity of European nations. Hatred, particularly hatred of other nations, he regarded as unworthy of the educated man. But such a detachment may become dangerous if it assumes that the educated classes of other countries are equally devoid of hate.

Meanwhile, having been returned to Parliament by the electors of the Combined Universities, Fisher resumed office as President of the Board of Education in Lloyd George's second Coalition, and during the next four years he had a somewhat wider sphere of public activity, as he was free from the labours of his Education Bill. In the Commons he frequently deputised for the secretary of state for India, and he helped Mr. Montagu in the drafting of the Montagu-Chelmsford Report, which sought to apply Liberal principles to the administration of India. At the same time he accepted a greater measure of responsibility for Irish questions. On the subject of foreign public opinion he was recognised in the Cabinet as an authority, and in February, 1919, he was consulted about those British academies abroad, notably in Athens and Florence, which might serve as agencies of 'propaganda.' Disliking intensely this subordination of literary or archæological institutions to political purposes, he suggested that the Foreign Office was more concerned in the matter than the Board of Education, but he recorded, with some distress, that opinion in Italy had taken a violent anti-French and anti-British attitude, and that measures there would be necessary to counter renewed pro-German activities. Accordingly, he thought that the British Institute at Florence should be subsidised, and that the *Corriere della Sera* should be supplied with articles depicting the English point of view. In Finland our efforts were impeded by the fact that the enemy had arrived there before us, and even the English grammars sold to Finns had been compiled by Germans who, it was clear, had nothing to learn from us in the art of educating foreign opinion.

Greece was another problem. On the grounds of 'self-determination' and because of 'the prospect of a long peace which lies before us' Fisher recommended the cession of Cyprus to our recent and unwilling ally. The majority of the inhabitants of Cyprus, as he pointed out, were Greek, and this voluntary cession would

' strengthen our moral prestige in the world. . . . Here is a chance of attacking the legend of British pharisaism; by this sacrifice we would strengthen our position in any attitude we might take regarding French interests in Syria, Greek interests in Macedonia, and the American interest in Ireland.' Thus spoke the Gladstonian Liberal. But a reputation for hypocrisy is not easily lost, and is certainly not dispelled by impulsive acts of generosity, which some foreigners, if they put no worse construction on them, regard as proofs of weakness or folly. Fortunately, the Government decided that we should retain Cyprus, because, though Greece at the time was friendly, no one could say in whose company she might be found in twenty or thirty years' time. Moreover, the large Moslem population of Cyprus was opposed to a change of sovereignty.

Meanwhile the centre of gravity had shifted to Paris and Versailles where, in Fisher's opinion, the atmosphere of peace-making was vitiated by a spirit of grab and by the evil conduct of a section of the Paris Press. In the actual negotiations he took no part, except for a consultation in May, 1919. In that month the German delegation pressed for a mitigation of terms, and Mr. Lloyd George summoned nine members of the Cabinet, including Fisher, and all the Dominion Premiers to a meeting in Paris where it was agreed to advise the Prime Minister to ask for certain concessions to the Germans, notably in the reduction of the period of armed occupation, and in the modification of the new frontiers in Eastern Europe whereby, it was urged, Germany should retain districts having predominantly German population. It was on this last point that Fisher may have influenced his colleagues. He pleaded for more elasticity in the eastern frontiers, and he was drawing on his historical knowledge when he declared that ' a big Poland is necessarily a weak Poland.'[1] These recommended concessions at the expense of Poland were not well received by Mr. Wilson, who had a large Polish clientèle in the United States.

Though he was not a negotiator, it is not unlikely that Fisher through his close contact with Lloyd George had some influence on the spirit of the Treaty. On the one hand, the Treaty was imposed, not negotiated, because the peace-makers at Versailles believed that the war guilt was Germany's, and they held that guilt of such

[1] D. Lloyd George, *The Truth About the Peace Treaties*, pp. 688 ff.

dimensions should be punished; on the other hand—and here an academic or Liberal element can be detected—the Treaty was less concerned with safeguards for enforcing its terms than with the enunciation of exalted principles, such as those embodied in the Covenant of the League of Nations (an integral part of the Treaty) intended to provide for a better Europe, by which Germany herself would benefit. Mr. Lloyd George[1] declared that all the vocal criticisms of the peace terms, in England as in France, were in favour of harsher terms than those actually imposed, and in this respect the British delegation may have exercised a moderating influence, such as Fisher had always advocated; indeed, the pacification was regarded by the Premier and his political sympathisers as a triumph for Liberal principles, as evidenced by the creation of the League of Nations and the provisions for disarmament and for the rights of small nations. Opinion among other political parties was not unanimous, some Conservatives believing that the Treaty was rather harsh, while some Labour leaders maintained that it was vindictive, and was wrong in assuming the war guilt of the enemy.[2] Mr. Bonar Law objected that the settlement cut down too drastically the number of the German armed forces, and at one point in the negotiations Mr. Balfour, concerned perhaps about the survival of Teutonic culture, expressed some solicitude lest Germany should be left open to invasion. Fisher had no doubt that the Treaty was just. He thought it ' radical and democratic ':

> 'Poland, Czechoslovakia, Latvia and Estonia won their independence. Only six per cent. of European population was left under alien rule. If it be just that peoples should live under governments of their own choosing, then the map of Europe as drawn up at Versailles was the best map Europe has known.'[3]

These words probably provide the most convincing defence ever enunciated of the spirit of the Versailles settlement. But, while there

---

[1] *Ibid.*, p. 434.

[2] The late Viscount Snowden in his *Autobiography* referred to the 'outrageous penal terms of the Treaty' (p. 513), and to ' the falsehood that Germany alone was responsible for the war ' (p. 523).

[3] *Background and Issues of the War* (1940), p. 7.

were such wide differences of opinion about the justice of the Treaty, there appears to have been complete unanimity in the assumption that Germany would abide by its terms.

Second only in importance to the peace negotiations was the problem of Ireland. Those who accept the Marxian or economic interpretation of history may experience difficulty in explaining why, in spite of the steady alleviation of the Irish agrarian situation, the history of Ireland became more violent and more tragic than anything in the experience of Gladstone or Parnell. In the attempt 'to kill Home Rule by kindness' the Balfour administration had introduced measures which in course of time were bound to transform a peasantry into a society of small proprietors, and it may be hazarded—if anything can be hazarded about Ireland—that economic grievances were singularly absent from the rebellion of Easter Week, 1916. There was, it is true, a Labour Party in Southern Ireland but, more important, there was a Hierarchy which ensured that Irishmen would not join forces with foreign communists, and meanwhile the land reforms had created a rural middle class which provided the backbone of the nationalist movement. Sinn Fein was already well organised; the revival of the Irish language, originally a literary movement, was now an inspiration for the cause of separatism: and the war, which to many seemed Ireland's opportunity, helped to create that atmosphere in which violence and destruction appear normal things. There can even be detected a disturbance in the ordinary sense of values, to which humanity has since had to become habituated, a disturbance noticeable in unexpected places, as in the wording of a joint pastoral issued by the Irish Clergy from Maynooth in October, 1922: 'In this lamentable upheaval the moral sense of the people has, we fear, been badly shaken. We read with horror of many *unauthorised* murders.'[1] Fisher, it need hardly be said, knew little of Ireland; to him, as to many Englishmen, it was more foreign than any Continental country.

Gladstone's Home Rule policy had been based on a genuine concern for grievances of Ireland, but his two Bills served only to weaken the Liberal Party in favour of the Conservatives, and to add one more element, and an embittered one, to the struggle—Protes-

[1] Quoted in W. A. Philips, *The Revolution in Ireland*, p. 292.

tant Ulster. Where Gladstone had failed it was probably impossible
for any Englishman to succeed. Asquith's Bill of 1912 was placed
on the Statute Book under the provisions of the Parliament Act,
which was passed mainly in order to give effect to the Home Rule
measure. Meanwhile, the gun-running at Larne, together with the
language of Mr. Bonar Law and the conduct of Mr. F. E. Smith,
reflected a certain coarsening of English politics, mercifully
obscured for the time by the outbreak of the Great War, and so
the Bill of 1912 was suspended. By the last year of the war the
situation was even more complicated than before. Asquith had given
two pledges—that Ulster would never be coerced, and that Ireland
should have what she had been demanding for over thirty years,
namely, a national parliament for the whole country. These two
things might be reconcilable in transcendental metaphysics but not
in twentieth-century Ireland; accordingly, the older generation of
Irish politicians was classified according to which 'pledge' was
insisted upon, while the younger generation rejected both. On the
suggestion of Mr. Lloyd George a convention of representative Irishmen was summoned to discuss and determine among themselves
how the problem of Irish self-government should be settled; they
held their sessions between June, 1917, and April, 1918. But they
failed to arrive at any constructive agreement, a minority recommending a scheme of Dominion Home Rule, while a majority
favoured a more limited form of autonomy, in which the powers of
the Irish legislature did not extend to foreign relations or to
questions of peace and war. A committee of the Convention
reported against conscription. It was a misfortune for Ireland that
John Redmond died at this time. But even thus, these proceedings
were of little more than academic interest. The majority of the
delegates represented an older and more responsible generation, and
the Ulster representatives assumed throughout that there was no
question of their having to submit to an all-Ireland Parliament
sitting in Dublin.

The worsening of the situation, even during the few months of
the Convention's sessions, was reflected in April, 1918, when Lord
Wimborne was replaced by General Lord French as Lord Lieutenant. The threat of conscription served the turn of the younger
hot-heads, not all of them of the male sex, but all of them deter-

mined to repudiate even the most nominal subordination to the Crown, and to create an independent Irish Republic. German money and propaganda had been by no means wasted on the more unscrupulous, and Southern Ireland was dangerous not because of poverty (which had greatly diminished), but because of hatred. In the background was the Hierarchy, secretive and resourceful, openly contemptuous of what they considered the amateurish strategy of English statesmen, most of whom appeared as bland and genteel as the columns of their daily *Times*, all of them (except Mr. Lloyd George) unable to understand why they were so detested in the sister isle.

In January, 1919, the first Dail Eireann met. Its president, Mr. De Valera, could not attend, as he was in an English gaol, a fact which gave to the proceedings of the diet the fervour of a faith. That faith became a crusade when in September of the same year the Dail Eireann was prohibited and suppressed as a dangerous assembly. Of the resentment aroused by British attempts at suppression, there is a hint in the words of a letter written in April, 1920, by Erskine Childers to Fisher, who had intervened on behalf of a friend of Childers arrested on suspicion:

'You say there is a dilemma, one horn of which is that there must be arrest on suspicion. I beg of you to dismiss that belief.... It makes one sick—neighbours encouraged to spy and lie about one another on a stipulation that they need not give evidence in public. But the whole practice is barbarous? And why? Because the whole of the regime in Ireland is revoltingly barbaric. Prussian is a feeble name for it. You cannot stamp out a huge, popular democratic sentiment like this. All you can do is to degrade yourselves and the subject peoples in the effort. I know no blacker sin under God than what is going on here. I served four years in the War under the belief, growing ever fainter but held to the end, that it was fought to make such things impossible, and now I am daily witness to the prostitution of the Army I served in to fulfil the many aims I loathed and combated. I am Anglo-Irish by birth. Now I am identifying myself wholly with Ireland, which was for long my home in youth. But I still love England, and every minute's work I do is done not only to free Ireland, but for the sake of England herself, for disruption and decay will inevitably follow with the British Empire, as with

every other since the world began, from the futile suppression of
subject nations. Thanks again for your action and letter.'

Something of the tragedy of Ireland can be discerned in this
letter from one of the most gifted and ill-fated of all who have
mingled in that tragedy, and Fisher was deeply touched by it.

These statements are intended to suggest that there was a certain
element of unreality about a measure with which Fisher greatly
concerned himself—the new Government of Ireland Bill, introduced
to the Commons in December, 1919. To the President of the Board
of Education was allotted the ungrateful task of piloting this Bill,
which he had helped to draft, through a half-empty House of
Commons. The 'Partition Bill,' as it was called, recognised the
rights of the Protestants in the six Ulster counties while ignoring
the rights of the Protestants in the South. On the two parliaments
in Dublin and Belfast were conferred extensive powers which stopped
short of treaties, war and peace, the armed forces, customs and
excise, merchant shipping and trade outside Ireland. A Lord
Lieutenant was to embody the supremacy of the Crown. While
the Bill was based on the principle that there are two Irelands, each
entitled to plead the doctrine of self-determination, an attempt was
made to pave the way for ultimate union by the creation of a council
or senate, in which Ulster and Southern Ireland were equally represented, to which the two parliaments might, by agreement, transfer
any or all of their powers. Forty-two Irish members were to sit at
Westminster. Fisher believed that the Bill was the wisest possible
in the circumstances, because the two main interests concerned
received a large measure of satisfaction, and the measure provided
machinery which, if properly utilised, might introduce unity by a
process of 'gradualness.' His only objection was that the Bill by
denying fiscal autonomy did not go far enough, and offered no more
than a Crown Colony type of government. But he and his colleagues
were soon to realise that, while they had placated Ulster, they had
made no impression whatever on the lawless and fanatic element
which had now displaced Dublin Castle in the rule of Southern
Ireland.

The fate of this measure proved to be one of Fisher's many
political disappointments. In May, 1921, the Bill came nominally

into force, with the Roman Catholic Lord Fitzalan as the first Viceroy, but only a month before the 'Black and Tans' had been instituted to do the work of the Royal Irish Constabulary, and for some time the state of Southern Ireland had been one of civil war. In May there was a sweeping victory for Sinn Fein at the elections, and by the end of 1921 the problem of Southern Ireland had been narrowed down to this unanswerable question—how could Irish national aspirations be combined with the Imperial connection? 'Given an all-Ireland parliament the Republicans might accept Crown and Empire; given Crown and Empire the Ulstermen might accept an all-Ireland parliament '[1]—such were the slender hypotheses between which the Irish question was precariously balanced. An apparent solution was reached by the treaty of December, 1921, whereby Ireland was given the same status as Canada, and was to be known as the Irish Free State, with an explicit retention of the Imperial connection and the supremacy of the Crown. To the House of Commons this was proclaimed a victory for the Coalition's Irish policy, while to Griffith and Collins, the Irish agents, it was represented as a great concession at the expense of Britain, and so it appeared that the faces of all parties had been saved. From this arrangement Ulster was given the option of contracting out, an option which she promptly exercised. In more devious ways Eire also 'contracted out.' Her independence was made practically complete when she received the naval bases by a British concession which, it was hoped, would encourage Irish confidence in English good faith, a highly moral object lesson, destined in the Second World War to cost the lives of many British seamen. It was probably the Irish trouble which wrecked the Coalition, but it may be doubted whether any government could have achieved a settlement capable of maintaining Eire effectually within the British Dominions.

In addition to the increasing work of his department, a number of miscellaneous educational matters engaged Fisher's attention at this time. On May 19, 1920, at a dinner at the Guildhall he announced the Government's offer of the Bloomsbury site to the University of London, the acceptance of which eventually enabled the University to secure administrative centralisation for many scattered activities. He was also mainly responsible for another

[1] D. Macardle, *The Irish Republic* (1937), p. 584.

service to the University. A few days after the Armistice he dined with Haldane in order to meet Sir Ernest Cassel, who, it was understood, was anxious to give large sums for the cause of higher education. The results of the dinner-party were thus summarised:

> 'I secured £150,000 for a Faculty of Commerce in London, £150,000 for the higher education of women and £50,000 for the Workers' Educational Association. Cassel is a queer old German Jew, very shrewd, but simple and public-spirited. I like him, and he gave me a lift home in his brougham.'

There was a sequel eighteen months later when Fisher drafted for the King a speech to be read at the laying of the foundation-stone of the new wing of the London School of Economics which Cassel's benefaction, together with public subscriptions, had made possible.

Other ministerial duties at this time were not so spectacular. In the preceding February of this year he had been asked to enquire, in consultation with the ministers concerned, into the question of decontrol of food, a relaxation foreshadowed by the fact that the powers of the Ministry of Food were due to lapse in the following August. The bread subsidy was now costing 56 millions per annum, and there was apprehension lest, if the prices of essentials were allowed to rise, demands for increased wages would have to be faced. His reports indicated that there was no prospect of a fall in prices. Grain in Russia could not be moved to the ports; the United States, having gone 'dry,' was consuming more sugar, and the American packers who dominated the bacon market were likely to exploit their advantage to the fullest. Moreover, the acreage of home-grown wheat had diminished since 1918 by 400,000 acres, and it has to be recalled that the war-time measures for the increase of tillage had added no more than 37 days' supplies per annum. In view of these facts, Fisher and his colleagues recommended that some form of control should be retained, and that the Ministry of Food should be continued for another two years, if only to remind the public that the Government had extensive powers to check profiteering.

These domestic matters were overshadowed in importance by the international affairs which held the attention of the Government throughout the year 1920, and Fisher was soon to have an opportunity of gauging for himself the temperature of Europe in the years immediately following the war. The Treaty of Versailles had brought into existence the League of Nations, consisting of Council, Assembly and Secretariat. To the Assembly, which began its sessions in the autumn of 1920, were entrusted very large powers, for it might deal with any matter within the sphere of action of the League, or affecting the peace of the world; it regulated the admission of new members, elected the non-permanent members of the Council, and appointed the judges of the Permanent Court. The Assembly could also advise on the re-consideration of treaties which had become inapplicable, or the revision of international commitments which might endanger the peace of the world; in general, it was the directing body of the League, and by its annual review of work done in the preceding year it helped to provide some guidance for the future. Each delegation to the Assembly consisted of not more than three principal delegates. With Mr. George Barnes and Lord Robert Cecil, Fisher was appointed a delegate to the Assembly, Mr. Balfour being the British member of the Council. Barnes, a straightforward representative of Labour, was buoyant and ingenuous, sometimes a source of disquiet to his more sophisticated colleagues; Lord Robert Cecil, once described by an Irish member of parliament as 'having one foot in the Middle Ages and the other in the office of the League of Nations,' had all the piety and impenetrability of the House of Cecil, and was imperative in his demands for the vindication of strictly moral principles in public life; Mr. A. J. Balfour, legatee of the sagacity of the same House, and therefore much cooler than his cousin, regarded the progress of mankind as from one Ice Age to another, and may well have considered the League of Nations an elegant milestone in that inevitable, but dispiriting, pilgrimage. Religious fervour, transparent honesty, intellectual distinction and philosophic detachment, such were the qualities most obvious in the middle-aged and elderly members of the first British delegation to the League of Nations. But were these qualities quite enough? In December, 1918, General Smuts in a pamphlet had urged that if the League was to succeed it must be backed by the full strength of the governments concerned, and that consequently the Prime Minister or Foreign Secretary should on all important occasions attend the Council in person. On this important occasion, the start of the League's proceedings, Mr. Balfour was no adequate substitute for Mr. Lloyd George, and as for the other members, their personal eminence was so much more obvious than their political effectiveness that one is tempted to ask whether, even as early as 1920, the British Government really believed in the League.

General Smuts' pamphlet was one of the most remarkable documents of the Great War. Advocating a League having much wider powers and duties than had previously been suggested, Smuts contended that 'the progress of civilisation has always been towards the League of Nations,' as evidenced by the grouping of nations into great empires, which are embryonic leagues. Of these empires only the British Empire was actuated by a spirit of equity and freedom, the others, Russian, Austrian and Turkish, then in process of liquidation, having been autocratic and oppressive. The new League of Nations 'general heir or successor to the defunct empires' must, in its territorial policy, proceed on the axioms of no annexations and the self-determination of nations. 'Europe requires a liquidator or executor of the bankrupt estate, and only a body like the League can adequately perform that gigantic task.' The old Imperialism was to give way to a new world of freedom, for which purposes Smuts proposed that the Great Powers should, by a system of mandates, administer those constituent parts of the fallen empires which were not yet ready for statehood—the United States, for example, might administer Palestine; Great Britain Mesopotamia; and Albania might be entrusted to Italy, but such mandates were to be subject to the absolute control of the League. This conception of mandates was derived by General Smuts from his study of Roman Law, and it is noteworthy that neither Smuts nor any other influential contemporary even suggested the extension of the system to Germany, which, far more than Mesopotamia or Albania, needed wise direction from outside. Having outlined a scheme for the constitution and powers of the League, such as was afterwards in many respects put into effect, Smuts warned the readers of his memorandum against the assumption that the League would necessarily end war. It could, at best, make war less likely, by ensuring 'a breathing space before the disputants are free to go to war ... a binding moratorium, during which the parties to the dispute agree not to proceed to extremes, but to await the results of the enquiry to which their case has been referred.' The economic boycott of 'sanctions,' if effectively applied, might well, he thought, prove a deterrent; indeed, experience of the war just ended had shown how successful this weapon might be. Smuts was well aware of the human difficulties that would confront the new institution. In particular he was concerned about the ' Conference ' or ' Parliament ' of the League (the Assembly) which ' will have to be carefully chosen so as to make it a useful body, and to prevent it from being looked upon on the one hand as a futile debating society, and on the other as a dangerous body whose debates are likely to inflame the slumbering passions of the national populations.'

Both these forebodings were speedily realised. In a spirit of high hope and confidence Fisher and his colleagues went to Geneva for the first meeting of the Assembly of the League in the autumn of 1920, when the main questions to be discussed were the Polish-Dantzig dispute, disarmament, and intervention against Turkey on behalf of Armenia. It was not long before a note of disappointment crept into Fisher's record of the proceedings; indeed, from the outset he found the League a Grand Sanhedrin of chatter and typescript. Thus, of the proceedings of the committee on armaments he noted ' huge speeches fired off by the South Americans without any result.' Nor were the Latins the only offenders in this respect, for in November Mr. Balfour had to undertake the invidious duty of hinting to the Dominion and Indian delegations that they were talking too much. There was repeated and acrimonious disagreement between the British (especially Lord Robert Cecil) and the French, due not so much to differences of opinion, as to racial and personal antagonisms on remote questions which might have been settled by correspondence. Fisher had to fight the French over the demand that their Polish protegés should be given an exclusive mandate for Dantzig, as later he had to fight them over measures for the control of the drug and the white slave traffics (in this contest he was forced to the conclusion that the French had some obscure interest in these traffics, possibly on account of their black troops); frequent verbal duels between A. J. Balfour and Viviani on the subject of Turkey's conduct in Armenia had no other result than the formation of a committee to mediate with Kemal on behalf of the Armenians ('I fear that things don't look very hopeful for the Armenians,' wrote

Fisher); even the Dutch delegates were influenced by Imperial pre-possessions, and were unwilling to come to the support of Armenia because, as they had over forty million Moslem subjects in Java, they were anxious not to cause displeasure to the Turk. Everyone seemed in favour of admitting small nations to the League, and from the start British Labour was anxious to see the admission of Germany.

These national differences were most obviously reflected in the debates on disarmament. The French were opposed to it, because they were convinced of two things—that Germany was not completely disarmed, and that sooner or later she would again be fully armed for more aggression. To many Englishmen, as to the Dutch and Scandinavians, the French attitude appeared both unreasonable and incomprehensible; hence their whole-hearted enthusiasm for general disarmament, now that Germany, repenting her war guilt, was (they thought) harmless and reformed. Indeed, some Anglo-Saxons, influential and idealist, were convinced that France was likely to prove the militarist and aggressive nation, and that German civilisation must at all costs be preserved from that threat. In the British delegation there was unanimity about disarmament, but difference of opinion about its method. Lord Robert Cecil, in his headlong manner, wanted disarmament by a general treaty, while the more moderate Fisher, anxious to find a 'formula' which would satisfy both French and Scandinavians, was in favour of regional agreements. The first was thought dangerous because too sweeping; the second, it was feared, might lead to the formation of territorial or political groups. But these differences faded away when, at the Third Assembly in 1922, it was suddenly realised that an essential preliminary to disarmament is a sense of security; so for this purpose a treaty of Mutual Assistance was drafted whereby the Council was authorised to apply 'sanctions' where there was a threat of war. This treaty was rejected by the British Government.

But Fisher was not distressed by these things. He at first enjoyed the variegated scene at Geneva, and wrote that he would be happy 'if it were not for Ireland.' He saw much of the social life in the Swiss city, a city which, in the words of Sir Alfred Zimmern, became 'something between a market-place, a public meeting and a revivalist place of worship.'[1] On Sundays Mr. Balfour read the lessons

[1] Sir. A. Zimmern, *The League of Nations* (1936), p. 292.

in church, while Fisher went for a walk or read Livy in his room. Brilliant dinner-parties were frequent. A dinner with Ranjitsinjhi in December, 1920, is thus described:

'Ranji's dinner was small, select and most luxurious. Ali Iman, who is Prime Minister to the Nizam, discoursed to me on the necessity of making the Nizam a king. A Spanish guest gave an extraordinary account of Trotsky's descent on Barcelona and of his organisation of revolutionary movements there. Ranji discoursed economics to be effected in the League (he has become a stern economist in public, though not in private expenditure). A. J. B. beamed pleasantly on everybody.'

This was followed a few nights later by another party:

'Dined with the Japanese last night. Very pleasant dinner. They *are* intelligent. Ishii very curious about Bertrand Russell, who is apparently going to lecture in Japan. Was he not very dangerous? Unfortunately, after dinner old Doherty, an Irish Canadian, lectured us interminably on the Irish question, and I didn't get away till after midnight.'

Ireland, the only occasion of anxiety to Fisher in these days, may also have been a subject of some interest to the 'intelligent' Japanese.

Returning to London late in December, 1920, Fisher found that increasing unemployment was providing anxiety to the Cabinet, and early in 1921 he urged that a solution could be found only in the application of Free Trade principles. Unemployment he attributed not to increase of foreign imports, but to lack of foreign orders, owing mainly to impoverishment of continental countries. The cure of the disease, he thought, was not the exclusion of those imports which were favourably affected by the exchange, but the encouragement of imports from, and the provision of sterling credits to, those countries which were once large customers for our goods. The workers in the boot trade, for instance, who used to sell their boots to Germany, knew that every order given by an Englishman for German brushes was a potential order given by a German for English boots. But in the new Europe which was shaping such an argument sounded out-of-date, and soon, with the advent of Dr.

Schacht, there were to be devised more subtle methods for obtaining boots without having to part with brushes. Against the policy of 'safeguarding of industries,' Fisher pleaded for more liberal and far-sighted measures, such as fixing the German indemnity at a moderate amount, stabilising the Austrian exchange under a scheme intended to balance revenue and expenditure in that country and to prevent the further issue of Austrian paper money. But even these reasonable proposals were inapplicable in the changed order of things. By August, 1922, Britain had lent more than 12 millions to Austria (in addition to other Allied loans), and at that date Baron Franckenstein applied to Mr. Lloyd George for more, on the ground that the bankers would make no further advances without an Allied guarantee. Failing this, stated Franckenstein, the Austrian government would disintegrate, and the Entente Powers would be morally responsible for the collapse of one of the most ancient centres of civilisation. Mr. Lloyd George, on behalf of the Allied governments, refused the request, because repeated foreign loans had effected no improvement in the Austrian financial situation, 'which had gone from bad to worse.' But it was agreed to refer the matter to the League of Nations, and under the auspices of that body a 'loan' was afterwards floated.

The achievements of the League were the subject of a report by Fisher in July, 1921. The dispute over the Aaland Islands had been settled in favour of Finland; atrocities committed in Albania by Greeks and Serbs had been referred to the Council of Ambassadors; the Polish-Lithuanian dispute was prejudiced by the fact that Polish troops were still in Vilna; but on the other hand, as France was now aware of the shortcomings of the Poles, she was unlikely to give them any further countenance; Germany had complained of incidents in the Saar, but the French chief of the commission of occupation was showing a spirit of conciliation, and improvement would be effected when France removed her black troops; as regards Dantzig, the French, reported Fisher, were still 'foolishly apprehensive' of a German attack on the city, but otherwise, mainly through the instrumentality of the League, there had been progress in the settlement of differences between Poland and Dantzig. In August, reporting on the work of the Arms Traffic Commission, Fisher was obliged to offer equally lukewarm assurances to his col-

leagues. This commission was acting under a convention signed at
St. Germain on September 10, 1919, which prohibited the importa-
tion of arms and ammunition into Persia, Arabia, zones of the Red
Sea and Persian Gulf and certain parts of Africa. The only states
which had ratified the convention were Chile, China, Greece and
Siam. Such were the bases of European peace in the summer of
1921.

In the autumn of the same year the British delegation to the
League consisted of Mr. Balfour, Lord Robert Cecil, Mr. Fisher and
Sir Rennell Rodd, an ex-ambassador. The substitution of Rodd for
Barnes did not commend itself to all the other members, and Fisher
noted in his war diary that he was looking forward to the meetings
with apprehension, due partly to fatigue, and partly to the fact that
he dreaded the reference of important questions, such as that of
Silesia, to a League which did not include Germany. On his way
to Geneva he called in Paris on M. Millerand (M. Briand being
absent) in order to broach the subject of Germany's admission. M.
Millerand opposed the suggestion on the ground that the German
Government was too insecure, and had not yet fulfilled its obligations. Geneva provided further disappointments. September 5 he
noted as 'a very queer day':

'9.30 a.m. Armaments Commission. I had drafted an opening
to the report. Viviani made an eloquent but very silly speech in
criticism of it, objecting to my saying that the disarmament of
Germany was satisfactory, and objecting also to my expressing a
very mild hope that the Washington Conference might result in
a naval entente between the big powers. The French are too
prickly for words. In the afternoon we elected a Dutchman as
President, and he will make a very good one. The French voted
against him because the Kaiser is in Holland. The Swiss Federal
Council idiotically forbade either of the Swiss delegates to be
elected. Continual jealousies, I am told.
'A.J.B. in admirable form at dinner—talked of Browning,
Dizzy and Gladstone.'

But it would be unfair to quote further, because Fisher's letters at
this period show that he was a tired man, beginning to be disillu-
sioned. He was not 'wearing' nearly so well as Mr. Balfour, who,
after all, had had so much more experience of public life.

These proceedings were not without their effects on Fisher's health. He had a return of the old gravel trouble; he suffered from neuralgia, and he wrote to Lloyd George that he found international politics as practised at Geneva bad for the nerves. He confessed that the Assembly of the League was ' no more than a debating society, and not even a good debating society at that.' He still, in spite of much disappointment, believed in the League as the only bulwark between Europe and anarchy, but that was before the resurgence of Germany, Italy and Japan, and before the emergence of acute differ- ence of opinion within the League itself made it still more doubtful whether that organisation could ever command the whole-hearted support of any but the smaller powers. He worked hard in these early years to secure the admission of Germany, and though he doubted whether America would give up her isolation, he was fore- most among those who desired to improve our relations with the United States. When Sir Edward Grey retired from the ambassador- ship in Washington, there was a general feeling that Fisher should succeed him, but the Prime Minister had evidence that the teachers were anxious to retain their President of the Board of Education, and so Fisher just missed a unique opportunity of exercising his great powers of diplomacy.

The year 1922, Fisher's last year of office, was one of difficulty and disappointment. In the earlier months he was seriously con- sidering resignation, but he stayed on in the hope of saving as much as possible from the Geddes Axe. In March and April there was some alarm about the development of the French Air Force, and Fisher thus expressed his anxiety :

' France is very formidable, far more formidable should she ever quarrel with us than ever before in history. I never breathe a word of this, but one cannot help feeling that France has made herself sufficiently strong to snap her fingers at any kind of diplo- matic pressure from us.'

Apparently Renan, and his words about *la France qui meurt*, had been forgotten. These fears persisted throughout the summer months of 1922, but at least there was the consolation that Germany was (presumably) disarmed, and opinion might move in favour of her admission to the League. In September, at Geneva, Fisher interviewed Bernstorff, head of the German League of Nations Union, who expressed the view that the best chance of a strong government lay in alliance between Stinnes, the great shipowner, and the leading industrialists. Bernstorff told Fisher that the most influential literature in Germany was Bolshevik, but this in his opinion was no great matter since the Army could, if necessary, put it down. He regretted that ' no promising young man ' was coming forward.

The ' promising young man ' was on his way.

At home there were signs that the Coalition was not likely to survive the year. The Tory back-benchers were becoming increasingly restive; unemployment was extending, and the Irish ' problem ' was even more acute than before. Events in the Near East, where Lloyd George favoured the Greek movement against Mustafa Kemal, provided a good pretext for turning out the Government, since it could be argued that the Prime Minister's hellenist sympathies might lead to another war. On October 4, 1922, Mr. Lloyd George, in pessimistic mood, talked of a general election at once, with his own retirement to follow. He was convinced that most of the Liberal seats would be captured by Labour and that, in his own words, ' Liberalism was done for.' But with a statesmanlike instinct for terminology he expressed a hope that, under another name, the party might just survive. He favoured the title ' Progressive,' a label already popularised in the municipal politics of London; under such a new and suggestive name, assisted by the support of moderate Labour, the old party might still endure. It seemed a sad end to the great traditions of Gladstonian Liberalism, but Mr. Lloyd George consoled himself and his Liberal colleagues with the reflection that after all, Gladstone was really a Celt, and had never been popular south of the Trent. He himself was willing to serve under Asquith, but that statesman had lost too much prestige by his conduct of the war, and as for Grey, he was now impossible, for he had recently been going about making silly speeches.[1] The future, according to the mercurial Premier, offered no brighter prospect than that of helping to keep in office that ' tired-out Tory ' Mr. Bonar Law. With these gloomy forebodings the Ministry resolved to accept the by-

[1] In a speech of January 22, 1922, Grey was reported as saying: ' it was absolutely essential to restore wholesome, straightforward politics in this country.' (*Annual Register*, 1922, p. 4.)

election at Newport as a test case, and when a Conservative was returned for that constituency (October 19) the Coalition accepted defeat and resigned. On October 19 there was a meeting which, in effect was a farewell party. Mr. Austen Chamberlain, in valedictory mood, extolled Mr. Lloyd George; Mr. Balfour said he had never known a more harmonious Cabinet; Lord Birkenhead, introducing a forensic element, rebutted the accusation (by whom not specified) that he was the Judas of the Cabinet, for, as he had always been faithful to Mr. Lloyd George, the opprobrious epithet could not properly be applied to him. Six days later the obsequies of the Ministry were celebrated in more ceremonial manner at the Palace, where the King expressed the opinion that the policy of his late Government in the Near East had maintained peace, and had secured the respect of the Turk. His Majesty congratulated Fisher on his work for the League of Nations, on his services to the cause of education and the cause of the teachers, and he expressed a sense of pleasure that, in a more public capacity, Fisher had served him as his father had served His Majesty's royal father when Prince of Wales.

VII

Out of Office: Warden of New College
1923–40

In the interval between December, 1922, and his election to the Wardenship of New College in January, 1925, Fisher had no official employment other than that of member of parliament representing the Combined English Universities, and in this period he supported himself and his family mainly by journalism. He had enjoyed his experience of public life; he loved the House of Commons, with its great traditions, already so familiar to him as a student; most of all, he had welcomed, in the Cabinet, close association with statesmen in whose hands had been placed the destinies of empires and continents. Now, at the age of 58, he was not only at the end of his political career, but seemed destined to outlive the great Liberal Party to which he had never failed in his allegiance. Had he been merely a clever politician he could, by going over to the Conservative or the Labour Party, have hoped again to have enjoyed office; or, had a Liberal government returned to power, he might well have gone to the Lords, to grace that chamber as an Elder Statesman. But other duties were in store for him, the fulfilment of which may constitute a better claim to the notice of posterity than even the great public services which he had already performed.

It was at the suggestion of Mr. Lloyd George that, late in April, 1923, he went unofficially to Berlin in order to explore German opinion regarding Reparations and entry into the League. He first saw Lord D'Abernon, the British Ambassador, who spoke freely on conditions in Germany as they were known at the Embassy. D'Abernon stated that he saw no sign of underfeeding among the populace, and he assured Fisher that Germany was now our friend in the East, since she was very unwilling to ally with Russia. German opinion about the occupation of the Ruhr was, he thought, divided, the Jews being for compromise, the Christians against; but the failure of the latter to do anything was accepted by the Embassy as

115

proof that the country was now completely disarmed. He thought that France would not have entered the Ruhr if Germany had been a member of the League, and he estimated that reparations of £1,750 millions could be paid. Fisher then interviewed Professor J. H. Morgan, a shrewd investigator on the spot, who did not share the optimism of Lord D'Abernon and his staff. Professor Morgan gave some disquieting news about disarmament.[1] Germany, he reported, was disarmed so far as munitions were concerned, but on the other hand she retained the *cadre* of a large army, for a corps of instructors was still in being, and reservists were subsidised by the Government. Large subsidies for the armed forces and the civil service provided one reason why the Weimar Government did not even try to balance its budget. The demand for reparations had served to centralise national finance, the government now exercising the right to raise loans in every state, and this in turn had caused a great increase in the number of Reich officials. Evasion of taxes was universal; falsification of accounts was frequent; the republican government was held in general contempt, and the nation was united in hatred of France, particularly for the 'black shame' of the Ruhr occupation, though it was admitted even by Germans that the black troops had not behaved badly. Since the end of the war, reported Morgan, there had been a great development of German internal resources. Everyone was extending his business; many new buildings were being erected, and the exchange rate was helping to develop an export trade. The nation had not forgotten Ludendorff's dictum that the two things which Germany would never tolerate are a republic and a volunteer army.

Such were the official and unofficial pictures of Germany in 1923 as presented to Fisher. But from a third source he received perhaps the most significant intimation. In a Berlin cinema he saw a film purporting to depict the military career of Frederick the Great, and he was impressed by the loud and prolonged applause when the screen portrayed another of the many resounding victories for Prussian arms. But Fisher still hoped that Germany would live down this perverted patriotism. Soon, however, there was cause for disquiet in another quarter, for in the summer of this year Mussolini appropriated Corfu, and an award of the Ambassadors' Conference

---

[1] See his book, *Assize of Arms* (1945).

practically condoned the act. Italy, as Fisher dolefully admitted, had defied the League, and defied it successfully; the British Fleet should, he thought, have been sent to the help of the Greeks. But, under pressure from Lord Robert Cecil and the League of Nations, Mussolini yielded, and Corfu was returned, an undoubted triumph for the League, but nevertheless a cause of some disquiet for the future. All this seemed no more than a *sequela* of war fever, and to Fisher, as to most of his contemporaries, it appeared that a sedative rather than a surgeon was what the restless patients of Europe needed. In August, 1924, he wrote in terms suggesting that he still believed in the League, in the following letter to Gilbert Murray, who, as one of the South African delegation to the League, was helping to raise the level of the Dominion contribution to that institution:

'I wish I could be with you at Geneva this year, for it looks as if the session would be interesting and important, but I am out of these things now, and Geneva will see me no more. I had a talk with Hymans the other day, and found him nervous about Security. He wrung his hands over Poincaré's rejection of Lloyd George's offer of a defensive pact, qualifying it as 'une faute énorme,' as indeed from the French point of view it was. I tried to tranquillise him, but the Belgians have received disquieting accounts of the temper of Germany, for which they have largely themselves to thank.

'If you get a chance of speaking soothing words at Geneva, they may do. It is largely a matter of nerves with the Belgians and the French. They greatly over-rate the preparedness of Germany for a new attack and their own defensive resources should an attack come. Also they are blind to the fact that the leaders of German opinion are dead against anything of the kind.'

From this it may be deduced that Fisher had adopted the views of Lord D'Abernon rather than those of Professor Morgan, and so, even thus early, Germany's visitors were reduced to 'guessing.'

Among Fisher's literary activities at this time (varied by regular attendance at the House) editorship played an important part. With Gilbert Murray and Sir Arthur Thomson he had for some time been a joint editor of the Home University Library, a series which, as the name implies, is intended to supply in condensed and easily-understandable form something of the disinterested instruction about science, literature, history and public affairs which a university might be expected to provide. Fisher, who always made it his business to know men of intellectual promise, was anxious to ensure that the series should have for contributors not only writers of established reputation in their subjects, but also young men who, though unknown, seemed capable of real literary achievement. In this respect his most notable choice was Lytton Strachey, whose first book *Landmarks of French Literature* was produced by the Home University Library in 1912. In the summer of 1923 Fisher was invited by Douglas Jerrold—afterwards to do so much in the designing of the plan for the *History of Europe*—to undertake a more difficult task, that of editing a new series, published by Messrs. Benn, entitled 'Nations of the Modern World.' Modelled on De Tocqueville's *Democracy in America*, the volumes were intended to provide 'a picture of each nation as it is now, with such historical explanations as are necessary to explain the political, social and intellectual forces which are still moulding the life of the people.' There was no doubt that the war had created an increased demand for such books. Jerrold made it clear that he did not want books by 'the ordinary English publicists who put out two or three books a year on the same or some analogous subject,' and accordingly Fisher had to find his contributors among eminent men known to be well qualified for the subjects allotted to them. This proved a serious difficulty. General Smuts declined the volume on South Africa in a letter which hinted that he could not turn his mind to literary pursuits while the state of Europe gave rise to such serious misgivings, and a similar fate attended the proposal that Mr. Winston Churchill should write the volume on the United States. But nevertheless the idea of the series was a good one, and twenty-four published volumes attest its successful fulfilment. Before long Jerrold was able to achieve a similar object by securing the services of his old Oxford tutor not as editor but as author.

Fisher's diary at this period is that of a spectator on the fringe of events, recording, usually in staccato phrase, his conversations and impressions. In October, 1923, he lunched with General Smuts, who said that Lloyd George was a genius, Mr. Baldwin he considered ' a nice gentleman, good for ordinary times, but not for these times.' The General had tried to impress on Mr. Baldwin that he and his party must abandon the policy of drift. Fisher retained his old intimacy with Mr. Lloyd George, and in January, 1924, the ex-Premier told him that Foch had had no general staff, even when commanding four million men, but only Weygand, 'a mild, lady-like little man, who was physically frightened of artillery, but knew where every wagon and man could be found.' Fisher may have accepted this statement with some reserve. Haig, according to Lloyd George, was a bad judge of men. Allenby and Maude, Mr. Lloyd George considered, had proved the best English generals in the war, and Plumer had been the best leader on the western front. A month later Fisher had a talk with Mr. Baldwin, who confessed that he was in a very difficult position—a prime minister without prestige, and 'a ready-made Cabinet with too many peers.' Moreover, he had to labour under the weight of a serious incubus, namely, Lord Curzon, without whom he might have been able to 'do something with the French.' In May, 1924, at a meeting of Liberals in Mr. Asquith's room Fisher stated that he was opposed to the idea of turning out Mr. Baldwin's government, but Mr. Lloyd George confessed that he was unable to vote for it.

' We decide to say nothing to the Tories, and leave them in suspense as long as possible. Asquith returns to the House and makes a splendid speech, chaffing the Tories for their miserable record, and indulgent to the Labour Party.'

Can it be wondered at that foreigners are unable to understand English politics?

In this year 1924 a welcome opportunity for another visit to the United States was provided by his appointment to deliver six lectures on the Harris foundation at Northwestern University, and his second invitation to give the Lowell lectures at Boston. Having now more time on his hands, Fisher decided to combine these duties with an extended visit to Canada, and with his wife and daughter Mary he left England on September 19, 1924. A brief stay in Montreal induced him to conclude that the city was really governed by the French Canadians, ' who have the voting power, though few of them are prominent in business.' Generally, he found a fatalistic view abroad that Canada was destined to be absorbed in the United States. At McGill he heard from Sir Arthur Currie the opinion that in Canada opinion was too sectional, and that the Dominion suffered from a paucity of university-trained men in the administration, as witnessed by the fact that so few of the Rhodes Scholars of British stock took any part in public life; indeed, from this point of view, Currie believed that the Rhodes foundation had proved a great disappointment. 'A French Canadian, applying for a Rhodes Scholarship, always says that he will go into public life: the English Canadian, never.' Fisher noted the elements of potential antagonism between the English and French populations of the Dominion, and in the maritime provinces he even found traces of separatist feeling. With Mr. Taft, then in Canada, he had conversation on a different topic. Taft expressed his conviction that President Wilson had really been opposed to the League of Nations, and that much of Wilson's policy had been dictated by anti-British prejudice; moreover, in Taft's opinion, America might easily have been brought into the League had Wilson thought fit to accept the Republican reservations. The result was that President Wilson had landed the United States in 'a humiliating position.'

Crossing into the States, Fisher's first recorded interview was with an American lady who said that the American soldiers had been disgusted, as the British soldiers had been, by the meanness of the French peasants. In October he was in Boston, the guest of an old friend and noted hostess, Mrs. Fiske Warren. His business was to give the second set of Lowell lectures, and it was inevitable that, like the Harris lectures, these should deal mainly with the problems of post-war Europe. Much of his information was derived from experience. He informed his audience that Wilson and Lloyd George had combined to oppose the French demand for the Rhine frontier, on the ground that to transfer more than five million Germans to French or international suzerainty would be contrary to the principle of self-determination. The French, said the lecturer, had made clear their conviction that possession of the Rhine bridgeheads was absolutely essential for their security, but against this it was argued at the Peace Conference that a Rhineland under foreign dominion would create a new international problem. 'The French say they are not secure, and I think they are right.' From Boston, Fisher proceeded to Washington, and on November 1 he was taken by the British Ambassador to interview the President, Mr. Coolidge, at the White House. Mr. Coolidge's conversation proved so tedious and lifeless that his visitors found it difficult to keep awake. 'By Jove, he's a dreary little beggar—a wonderfully undistinguished head of a great state.'

While his wife and daughter visited Winnipeg and Western Canada, Fisher followed out a lecture tour which included Cleveland, Princeton, Swarthmore, Ann Arbor, Buffalo, Ithaca, Syracuse and Cornell. For the most part the audiences were small, and the lecturer depended mainly on improvisations. While at Buffalo he was interested to hear that, mainly in consequence of his Education Act, there were about 100,000 'young persons' attending day continuation schools in New York State alone, and this may account for the fact that in some parts of the States Fisher was hailed as 'a kind of prophet.' He was impressed by the wealth of American universities, and at Princeton he admired 'a miniature Oxford, quadrangles, Gothic towers, oak-panelled halls, plots with sundials, all shining in this glorious and sweltering autumn heat.' He enjoyed the hospitality of many American hosts and hostesses, some of them old friends, some of them fellow-historians, all of them keenly appreciative of the distinction and grace which he brought alike to the lecture-hall and the dinner-table. But on his side Fisher was not enthusiastic about higher education in America as he saw it. It appeared to him top-heavy; entry into the universities was too easy; learning, heavily subsidised, became cheapened; the range of subjects was too wide, or rather the intellectual value of the subjects was not properly differentiated, and some colleges were really magnified high schools. He perceived what may happen to higher education if it becomes over-endowed, and if everyone, whether suitable or not, is paid to go to a university. On the other hand he had a very favourable opinion of the high level maintained by many American scholars in history and law.

This lecture tour had to be cut short by the fall of Mr. Ramsay MacDonald's short-lived Labour administration in October, 1924. Fisher keenly regretted this curtailment, as he had arranged to give a lecture in French at the University of Montreal early in December, and he was anxious to use what influence he had to encourage French

Canada, while remaining within the Empire, to preserve her distinctive culture and traditions. But as a general election was now at hand he decided to return to London. Meanwhile he drew up an election manifesto for the Combined Universities in which he expressed his belief that the best hope for Irish appeasement lay* in preserving the existing dualism 'until such time as Ulster comes in of its own accord.' As regards the Campbell case, which had figured so largely among the causes of the dissolution, he took a serious view of the alleged interference by politicians in the administration of justice, and he contended that the Labour party had been obliged to yield to pressure from the Left, as witnessed by the Russian Loan, the guarantee of which was an 'intolerable burden' on the British taxpayer. He ended with the criticism that the Labour Party had failed most of all in social schemes, notably in housing. 'Here in Canada,' he recorded, 'houses are rising everywhere, because Canadian bricklayers are unrestrained by trades unions. They lay six to eight times as many bricks as the English bricklayer, and they keep a Ford car.' The electors to whom these words were addressed again returned Fisher to Parliament.

But the remaining years of Fisher's life were to be connected not with Westminster but with Oxford. The venerable and beloved Dr. Spooner had announced his intention of retiring from the Wardenship of New College, an office which he had held with distinction for twenty-one years, and thus one more of the University's picturesque, now almost legendary, figures faded gracefully into seclusion. The Fellows of the College, the electors to the vacant office, had this difficulty that there were a number of its members who had a strong claim to election, but there was no doubt in their minds that on the grounds of public service and intellectual distinction Fisher was pre-eminent. Accordingly they elected him Warden in January, 1925. He was easily the most distinguished of all who had held that office since the foundation in 1379. Within a few months he gave up his seat in the House in order that he might be free to devote his whole time to the duties of his new post, and to Gilbert Murray he confessed that it was a great wrench to leave the House of Commons—'the mere atmosphere, contrary to the general opinion, is there so much higher and more serious than it is in a university, that is, if one considers the men who matter in the

House.' Of this unusual point of view he gave few hints to his colleagues.

The duties of his office were exacting and multifarious. He had to keep in close touch with a community of about 250 persons, and had to maintain open house for them and for old members of the College. He had to ensure that the fellows, tutors and officers of the College were adequately performing the duties assigned to them. For the management of the College estates he was directly responsible, and in this he was ably assisted by the wisdom and experience of both the Bursar and the Estate Agent. He was not obliged to teach, but of his own accord he took a number of the better pupils in 'Greats,' Modern History and the School of Social Studies. Correspondence on a large scale was inevitable, for he had been much in the public eye, and was therefore considered the right person to answer a great variety of questions, many of them showing a keen thirst for accurate information. A foreign scholar seeking the textual variations to be found in a Bodleian MS., an admirer of King Charles II anxious to know his exact height (surely such a popular king must have been tall?), an enquirer after the exact weight of Martin Luther (surely such a spiritual-minded man could not have weighed twenty stone?) and, most tiresome of all, a general reader wishing to trace a defective reference in a book written by an author too exalted in station to be approached on such matters, all these helped to swell the Warden's post-bag. His friendly relations with his colleagues enabled him to pass some of these enquiries to them. Throughout his fifteen years of office his ablest but least obtrusive lieutenant was his wife, on whose shoulders fell an unusually heavy burden of entertaining. It was she who helped to make the Warden's Lodgings a centre of hospitality not only for undergraduates and old members of the College, but for distinguished personages, and so this important side of Oxford life was more than maintained.

Fisher was the ideal head of a great college. Unlike a headmaster, who is answerable to a governing body meeting only at intervals, the head of a college is responsible to a body of persons, mostly adolescents, who are in residence during the greater part of the year. By temperament and by his historical loyalties Fisher was scrupulous of the niceties to be observed in this type of constitutional monarchy; solicitous of the rights of others, he never over-stepped his authority; too strong to be dependent on favourites, he was never captured by a clique; even more, his invariable efficiency was completely devoid of fuss or interference. But these are negative virtues, such as can be found in rulers who avoid mistakes. Fisher's personality was so striking that his presence alone was a stimulus. He endowed his office with such a dignity that even the most callow undergraduate, or the most fleeting member of the domestic staff, or the most deeply-rutted don was conscious of a higher standard and a greater purpose. He combined so many things usually dis-connected. He was aloof, but always accessible; a personage, some-times resplendent in the scarlet robes of his Oxford doctorate, or abounding in reminiscences of the Cabinet, but always human, and often genial. Pettiness and prejudice were unknown to him. His intellectual attainments and high character brought distinction not only to New College but to the University of Oxford.

Of his Wardenship the most tangible memorial is the new library, completed in 1940 from the designs of Mr. Hubert Worth-ington, an architect who has succeeded in the supremely difficult task of adding to Oxford buildings which have won the approval of academic connoisseurs. It was a great feat to erect between the mediaeval gothic of Wykeham and the victorian gothic of Sir Gilbert Scott a structure which at least preserves neutrality between the two opposed styles. The completion of this project, in what were to prove the last weeks of his life, was a great joy to Fisher, who had long set his heart on the object of replacing the cramped quarters of the old library by premises more worthy of the College store of books as well as more attractive to students. The new library, under the enterprising and devoted direction of the librarian, Sir John Myres, has achieved the feat of encouraging undergraduates to read more than they might otherwise have done. This important addition to the College buildings was made possible by the fact that there was in existence a fund, originally subscribed for the purpose of assisting the education of sons of old members killed in the war of 1914-8, and after all possible claims on that fund had been met there remained a residue which, with contribu-tions obtained by the Warden in this country, provided for the cost of the enterprise.

As *ex-officio* governor of certain schools and charities, including The Lord Williams Grammar School at Thame and the Grammar School at Bedford, the Warden seldom failed, even at some inconvenience, to attend meetings where his help in matters of policy and selection of staff was of special value. He had a singular felicity in interviewing candidates, whether for a scholarship, a professorship or a headmastership. With a minimum of words he could win the candidate's confidence, and elicit from him all that was relevant for the purpose on hand; he then presented to his fellow-electors a *résumé* of his own impressions, with some directions as to the type of person required for the post or the emolument, and how far each of the candidates had, in his view, conformed to that type. His invariable detachment and wide range of perspective gave confidence as well as guidance to his co-electors who, even when they did not agree, felt that at least Fisher had clarified the situation, and had reduced the problem to clear-cut issues between which they could choose. Of this mentality, which combined the judicial with the sympathetic, and took both the long and the generous view, Fisher was one of the best exponents in his generation. On the other hand, he was not always a shrewd judge of men.

His responsibility for the College property and estates involved an annual summer Progress, in which he was accompanied by one of the Fellows. The Progress, a mediaeval institution, was the visit of the lord of the manor to those tenements and lands where he had seignorial rights. His steward of the manors held courts, while the Warden inspected woods, crops and premises; he received hospitality, and he established personal, usually friendly, contact with the tenants. By 1925 the Progress had been shorn of much of its old consequence, because Lord Birkenhead's Act, by making the enfranchisement of copyhold compulsory, transformed into freeholders the comparatively small body of copyholders who still survived; consequently Fisher, unlike his predecessors, held no courts. But nevertheless the Progress had long been a means whereby landlord and tenant, by personal contact, had been better able to appreciate each other's point of view, and so the institution was retained. Fisher never claimed to have expert knowledge of farming, but he was familiar with the countryside, and he liked country ways and country people, consequently he valued this part of his duties; and though his diplomacy in such matters as reduction of rent or outlay on ambitious extensions of buildings was not so subtle as that of his revered predecessor, he nevertheless achieved a just balance between the needs of the tenant and the resources of the landlord, so that the College retained its high reputation as a corporate landowner.

For business purposes he kept a record of proceedings on Progress, and these sometimes throw light on agricultural conditions, mainly in Oxfordshire, Buckinghamshire, Berkshire and Essex in the years after 1925. He noted with regret that in the villages cricket was being displaced by lawn tennis. Among the farmers the most usual complaint was the great rise in costs; thus, on one farm where it had long been usual to give each labourer a gallon of beer each day, the price had risen from 7d. a gallon to 2/7. Sheep-shearing, formerly 3/6 per score, was now 10/-; a monthly blacksmith's bill of 30/- had become £5; in one case pre-war rates of 6d. had risen to 6/-. But in spite of all this the Warden occasionally met a farmer who had no complaints to make, for instance this one in North Oxfordshire:

> 'An excellent young man who served in the Oxfordshire Hussars all through the war, is now married, with a small child. Farms 110 acres, half arable, half pasture; keeps 71 cows, 110 lambs. Keeps two men. Says he has done very well, his buildings good, no complaint to make. Altogether thoroughly satisfied.'

Another good type, this time in Buckinghamshire, is thus described:

> 'An intelligent young man who has had a year's training at the Agricultural Department at Reading, from which he has profited, and has also held a commission in the 10th Hussars. He lost a hand two days before the Armistice. The manor farm is inhabited by his four sisters, all nice and busy, one an expert in poultry, another a kindergarten teacher in Buckingham, while he and his pretty young wife (educated at the Oxford High School) live in a smaller house in the village.'

To these official duties were added a great many voluntary activities. His membership of the Hebdomadal Council of the University enabled him to take an active part in the direction of academic policy. He was a leading spirit in the Oxford Preservation Trust which has done so much to preserve from desecration land and property in the vicinity of Oxford. As one of the Rhodes Trustees he was closely concerned with a great institution providing a personal link between Oxford and the Empire. Cecil Rhodes, one of the most visionary of our Empire-builders, had founded his scholarships mainly in order to bring the English-speaking races together, dreaming of an Anglo-Saxon empire of which, at one time, he thought Washington would be the capital. A number of the original scholarships were held by Germans, but these were suspended during the war of 1914–8. The Trustees were obliged to go to Parliament in order to secure an alteration in the terms of the Trust, mainly because the allocation of scholarships, as determined by Rhodes, was defective or based on an inadequate knowledge of the elementary facts of both American and Imperial development. On these matters Fisher gave evidence in March, 1929, before a committee of the House of Lords, and eventually a more equitable distribution was obtained. His colleagues of the Rhodes Trust greatly valued Fisher's services, not only because he combined a knowledge of the Universities with that of the Empire, but because of the detachment and wisdom which he invariably showed when co-operating with others. As a Trustee he had additional opportunities for seeing an old pupil whom he regarded with special esteem—Lord Lothian, who served as Secretary from 1925 to 1939.

Fisher's interest in all that concerned the Empire led him to take an active part in a scheme which unfortunately has not yet come to fruition. On the occasion of the Rhodes Memorial Lecture in 1929 General Smuts had made an appeal for the erection of a centre of African Studies in the University, on the ground that the future of Africa lay in the hands of a few European powers, and that intelligent administration of the continent must be based on wide knowledge. Accordingly he suggested that such a centre should be established in Oxford, based on Rhodes House, its funds to be administered by the Rhodes Trustees in conjunction with the University, the new centre to co-operate with an already-existing institution, the International Institute of African Languages and Cultures, in such a way that while the latter continued to specialise on the linguistic side, the new Oxford body would concentrate on the political, economic and scientific aspects of the African problem. This interesting proposal was quickly followed up and, together with a number of other prominent members of the University, Fisher interested himself in devising a scheme on the lines laid down by Smuts. The Hebdomadal Council approved the plan, and the Rhodes Trustees agreed to extend Rhodes House in order to accommodate the new institution. But, much to Fisher's disappointment, the project fell through from lack of funds. Few schemes could be more worthy of support than this one of better enabling us to fulfil our imperial responsibilities in Africa.

Such were the main Oxford activities of the Warden. In addition he performed a great number of services, many of them honorary, which brought him more perhaps than any other academic personage into contact with the public. Of these the one which provided clearest proof of intrinsic merit was that of Trustee of the British Museum. He appreciated few things so much as this opportunity of influencing the policy of one of the greatest institutions in the world, and here again his knowledge and experience were of exceptional value to his colleagues. This duty also provided him with a welcome opportunity of seeing more of his old schoolfellow Sir Frederic Kenyon, the distinguished Director and Principal Librarian of the British Museum. With somewhat less austere public bodies he was also associated. In 1932 he served as first chairman of the Central Council for School Broadcasting, and many of his suggestions, especially for the dramatisation of historical events, influenced later policy and programmes. From 1935 he was a Governor of the British Broadcasting Corporation. His colleague on the board, Mr. R. Norman, noted how willingly he acquiesced when the voting went against him; 'no doubt,' he wrote, 'Fisher was too deeply imbued with the central doctrines of Liberalism to despise the voice of the majority.' He was prompt to resist any threatened pressure from government departments, and for this reason he set himself against broadcasts in foreign languages for propaganda purposes, as such a policy would, in his view, entail some subordination of the Corporation to the Foreign Office. When war threatened in 1939 he took the lead among the Governors in resisting the proposal that the Corporation should be placed under the control of the Ministry of Information, declaring that 'the common danger to democratic civilisation at this time is the spread of machine-made government propaganda.' The reputation of the B.B.C. was, he held, due to the belief that it is independent of the Government; 'if the charter is suspended and the B.B.C. placed under a Ministry of Information, it is highly unlikely that the regime of liberty will ever be restored.' It was the last voice of Gladstonian Liberalism, resounding in a rapidly-expanding desert, and fortunately it was listened to. This was one of Fisher's best public services.

He was keenly interested in the immense possibilities of broadcasting. He knew its value as a means of adult education, as a guide to the young, as a solace to the blind, the lonely and the bed-ridden, and generally, as a means of supplying both enlightenment and entertainment to millions of very diversely-constituted people.

> 'Our general principle [he wrote] is to give to each section of the public the kind of thing it likes, but on a slightly higher level than that to which it has been accustomed. In that way we hope to raise the level of the community.'

Hostile criticism came, he thought, from those who listened-in only spasmodically, and had no idea of the range of appeal made by the B.B.C. 'I confess that until I became an invalid myself I did not realise how completely the ground was covered.' He was satisfied if he had thirty minutes' enjoyment a day from the wireless, and to the objection of Auckland Geddes that there was too much trash on the air he replied 'what is trash to Auckland Geddes may seem all right to less instructed listeners.' To other critics he had to provide the soft answer. A member of the public, infuriated by a neighbour's loudspeaker, was advised to consult a solicitor, because the B.B.C., while assuming responsibility for what was put into the ether, was not responsible for its volume at the other end. A clergyman, indignant that racing news was placed in close proximity with athletic events, had to content himself with the assurance that as there was now so much betting on football it was difficult to separate the racecourse from the playing field; nevertheless, he would try to keep them further apart. He attempted to soothe a distinguished historian who objected to the 'historical falsehoods' of Mr. G. K. Chesterton in a broadcast on 'Liberty.'

But, though hopeful that broadcasting would raise the level of public appreciation, Fisher had sometimes to confess that the process was slow and devious. With some more advanced movements he found himself out of touch. He disliked 'crooning'; he was too old-fashioned to find musical charm in the exuberant cacophony of muscular exotics, or in the tedious irrelevancies of those composers whose industry is worthy of a better cause; nor, as a mid-Victorian, could he appreciate the efforts of vocalists obviously unable to sing. In these matters he could exert no influence, so he held his peace. But in some other spheres he achieved results. Thus he successfully opposed the proposals that the Christian Scientists should be allowed to give a regular weekly talk, that they should broadcast their Sunday service, and that one of their representatives should have a seat on the religious advisory committee. He had no objection to the Christian Scientists stating their views, from time to time, on the air, but he clearly distinguished this from measures likely to imply that the movement was officially sponsored by the B.B.C. So too with the Oxford Group Movement (not to be confused with the earlier and quieter Oxford Movement), which had won over many souls of high social, athletic and academic standing, and wished to make full use of the exceptional opportunities for publicity provided by the wireless. Fisher, who had his views about the movement, saw to it that these opportunities were kept within reasonable bounds. He had the same scepticism about certain aspects of modern 'psychology' which emphasise the non-rational or sub-conscious elements in human nature, and under-estimate the forces of rational control. 'I hate psycho-analysis,' he wrote, when objecting to a proposed broadcast by an exponent of that art. Some will feel that in these matters Fisher was narrow-minded or out-of-date; others may conclude that he was exerting much-needed pressure on the side of public sanity and decency.

One of the most striking tributes to the public reputation enjoyed by Fisher is provided by the fact that he was invited to deliver, in the summer of 1930, the formal oration at the celebration in Boston of the tercentenary of the founding of the Massachusetts Bay Colony. Accompanied by his brother William, he went to Boston in July, and on the 15th of that month he delivered his address in the presence of an enormous gathering, attended by many notables, including ex-President Coolidge and the Governor of Massachusetts. Fisher excelled on occasions of this kind, and his speech, composed and delivered with his usual mastery, created an impression as favourable as that which he made personally in less formal contact with his hosts. Four years later he officiated with even greater *éclat* at another celebration—the fourth centenary of the landing of Jacques Cartier in Canada. On this occasion he was one of the two British representatives appointed by the Government, the other being Admiral Sir Roger Keyes. The French delegation was led by M. Flandin. The celebrations took place at Gaspé, and from the start there was a certain amount of apprehension lest complete concord might not prevail among the cosmopolitan gathering there assembled, and some of the speeches (most of them too long), where they did not indulge in platitudes, used phrases which might be considered patronising by the more sensitive French Canadians. There was also the difficulty of language. At last came Fisher's turn. He spoke in perfect French. He lightly disposed of the insinuation that French Canada was, after all, only part of a British ' colony.' On the contrary, England had embarked on her national greatness as a French colony, and turning to his neighbour Cardinal Villeneuve he reminded him of the Norman Conquest and what it had done for the insular English. He spoke with enthusiasm of the old and distinctive civilisation still perpetuated by the majority of his auditors, and how earnestly the Imperial Government desired that this civilisation should survive:

> ' Vous êtes le pays le plus libre du monde. Gardez avec soin votre civilisation française et vos libertés; l'empire britannique n'en peut rien craindre.'

The effect of the speech was spectacular. The band played the National Anthem, and everyone, including the Frenchmen, sang the words in French. ' Who is this Monsieur Fishère who speaks our language so beautifully?' was the question on many lips. He had saved the situation.

In January, 1936, he was invited by Dr. Murray Butler, President of the University of Columbia, to accept in person the honorary degree of Doctor of Letters ' on account of your distinguished official and educational services, and as a special tribute to your literally stupendous achievement—the *History of Europe.*' But owing to ill-health the Warden had to postpone his visit to the United States until the following year, when he received the honorary degree, and took advantage of the occasion to renew acquaintance with many friends in New York and Boston. Later in the same year (October, 1937) he was asked by a government department to give his opinion about the expediency of conferring on certain distinguished foreign potentates the degree of Doctor of Civil Law of the University of Oxford. It was a delicate matter in which Fisher's tact and experience counted for much. He had to point out that the honorary degree[1] was not conferred *in absentia*, and so, in the absence of the foreign ruler, it would be necessary for the Chancellor or Vice-Chancellor to travel abroad in order to confer the honour on its exalted recipient. Of those whose names had been suggested to him, it seemed to Fisher that the President of the United States was the least unsuitable. He thought it doubtful whether the University would approve of Mustafa Kemal, whose Smyrna atrocities seemed to suggest that, whatever he might know about Civil Law, he appeared to know little about human decency. ·Fisher also recalled that in a recent instance where the Oxford honour had been conferred on an oriental potentate, the degree had adhered too literally to his royal person, in the sense that the proud recipient, fascinated by his gorgeous scarlet robes, had insisted on wearing them all the way back to London.

This curious matter of the 'adherence' of an honorary degree was one in which Fisher himself was concerned, for in 1929 he had received from the University of Oxford the honorary D.C.L. At that time he was already the holder of several honorary degrees, one of them from Cambridge, but usually he had been known as 'Mr. Fisher' because, if the expression may be allowed, none of these doctorates had adhered closely enough to transform him into 'Dr. Fisher.' Would the Oxford degree succeed where the others had failed? Here was a problem of interest to conscientious students of our democracy. Some guidance is provided by the bishops, always the staunchest exponents of corporate consistency, for all bishops are Doctors of Divinity,[2] and the title of Dr. is not only adherent, it is inherent, for it is, as it were, kept in reserve beneath their outer

---

[1] As distinct from the degree by Diploma, which may be conferred *in absentia*.
[2] Whether of Lambeth or of a University, whether before or after consecration.

garments, as evidenced by the fact that, when divested of the name
of their diocese, they are seen to be clothed with a doctorate, and so
no right reverend person can ever be discovered in a state of social
nudity. But with right honourables and other highly-placed laymen
the position is somewhat obscure. It could not reasonably be expected that the admirals and generals who accept these academic
distinctions should surrender their existing titles for that of 'Dr.,'
or that they should try to utilise both; but with some statesmen,
where it might be thought that the plebeian 'Mr.' could easily be
exchanged for the higher title of 'Dr.,' it is noticeable that even
repeated applications of honorary doctorates appear to leave no impression whatever, and Mr. Lloyd George who, like Mr. Gladstone,
survived a heavy barrage of academic artillery, yielded up his 'Mr.'
only when he became an Earl. It would, in fact, appear that the
higher the status of a layman the less likely it is that an honorary
doctorate will adhere to his name, and this even serves to provide
a curious and unacknowledged criterion of a man's real reputation
with the public. Courteous friends, after Oxford had conferred its
honour upon him, addressed Fisher as 'Dr. Fisher,' somewhat to
his annoyance, for, as he explained to a correspondent, he had not
worked for the degree, nor applied for it; the doctorate was honorary,
'like that of Mr. Lloyd George.'

But there was no dubiety about another distinction conferred
on Fisher on the 1st of February, 1937—the Order of Merit. This
honour has been so carefully safeguarded that its award is recognised
as the clearest possible evidence of exceptional distinction in science,
in arts or in letters, and the many-sided achievements of Fisher made
him a specially worthy recipient of the Order. Moreover, as his
correspondence testified, the conferment of this signal honour gave
great satisfaction to a large public.

Across these fields of happy and fruitful effort there spread a
lengthening shadow—the situation in Europe. Fisher's public life
reveals the successive stages by which that shadow deepened. Late
in 1934 when refugees, many of them of high intellectual attainments, were beginning to come to England, an Academic Assistance
Council was formed, and Fisher was one of the many notable persons
who commended this cause to the public. An assurance was given
that the provision of academic posts in this country for displaced

foreign scholars would not in any way react on the prospects of our own students. But, while much good was done by this organisation, some could not help contrasting our immediate and enthusiastic response to the claims of foreign refugees with our almost complete indifference to the plight of those Irish loyalists who had been victimised by Sinn Fein, and in some quarters it was felt that too much emphasis was laid on the contention that the majority of the foreign intellectuals who came to our shores were irreplaceable. Fisher himself received evidence that the Academic Assistance Council was not approved by all who received its appeal. A copy addressed to an English graduate was opened in his absence by his mother, who, instead of forwarding it, wrote to Fisher a letter of protest, in which she recorded how her son, an ex-Service man, a distinguished scholar and winner of a research fellowship at Harvard, had been hit by the depression of 1931 and had now been three years out of work. He had been told by a professor to whom he applied ' that he could not find enough jobs for the Germans.' Fisher's reply is not on record.

There was also a division of opinion about another famous enterprise of the inter-war years. In 1935 were published the results of the Peace Ballot, and Fisher was one of the many influential men, including archbishops, bishops, statesmen and publicists, who expressed ' warm support ' of this curious experiment. The Ballot had the official approval of the Liberal and Labour parties, and owed much to the religious fervour of Lord Robert Cecil, who proclaimed his conviction that the League of Nations was in the direct line of Christian progress. Intended primarily to find out whether British opinion was behind the League, and to determine the principles on which European peace should be maintained, the Ballot provided evidence of increasing disquietude at the trend of international events, and was a pathetic attempt to establish popular confidence in an institution which appears never to have had the full support of the Great Powers. According to the promoters of the Ballot there were signs of increased vigour in the League:

> ' Intervention in the Saar, action on the Serbo-Hungarian dispute, insistence on a peaceful settlement of the Abyssinian difficulty are all welcome instances of the vigorous use of League machinery to solve international problems.'

In other words, the League was no longer what it had been when Clemenceau said: 'I like the League, but I don't believe in it.' The Ballot was intended to foster this apparently more favourable development, and to make clear to bewildered and anxious foreigners that Britain was solid for Peace and the League.

The Ballot had originated in an investigation into public opinion in Ilford in 1934. On the two questions whether Britain should remain in the League and whether the Disarmament Conference should continue there was an overwhelming preponderance of votes in the affirmative; but on the third question whether, in accordance with the terms of the Locarno Treaty, Great Britain should go to the help of France or Germany if one was attacked by the other there was an equally great preponderance of votes in the negative. To the organisers this vote on the third question was a keen disappointment, and various reasons were suggested to account for the unpopularity of Locarno—such as that there was a strong 'pacifist' element in Ilford, or, alternatively, that Locarno was black-balled because it was the achievement of a Tory government. Whatever may be the truth about these suggestions, the organisers were right in their conclusion that the question was too concrete, for it made explicit the contingency that, according to our diplomatic commitments, we might have to fight for Germany against France. In the rarefied atmosphere of the higher diplomacy there might seem nothing unusual about such a possibility, especially as it was an essential element in the 'interlocking' system whereby, it appeared, peace between the three Great Powers was assured; but, it may be suggested, to the workers of Ilford such an assumption, when clearly indicated, must have appeared absurd. After all, they and not Austen Chamberlain nor Herr Stresemann would have to do the fighting, and so their vote may well have been determined not by party politics, nor by 'pacifism,' but by indignant repudiation of a suggestion so preposterous as to be insulting. But this explanation does not appear to have occurred to the organisers of the Ballot, who determined to obtain the 'right' answer to their question. Accordingly, for the purposes of the national ballot, the troublesome third question was altered to this: 'Do you consider that, if a nation insists on attacking another, the other nations should combine to compel it to stop?' The result was a large majority of votes in the affirmative, and so the nation vindicated the cloudy and benevolent principles of 'collective security,' and at the same time proved that it is possible to obtain different answers to the same question provided its form is changed. Ilford had returned a clear answer to a clear question; the nation, presented with the same question in a form which left its full implications unexpressed, had given the opposite answer. Public opinion is often a matter not so much of thought as of terminology, and even the educated may be the unconscious victims of their own words.

More serious, the Peace Ballot—not through the fault of the organisers—created in many quarters the impression that to vote in a certain way was to decide for peace as against war, an impression strengthened by the title of a pamphlet issued in connection with the Ballot—*Peace or War*. From this, it was not difficult to reach the next stage—that an overwhelming vote in this country for peace would, in some way or another, procure European peace. Thus, a voter in Bedford told one of the callers that he had answered all the questions in the affirmative: 'it's him I'm thinking of,' he said, pointing to his small son. Nor was this view merely a misunderstanding to be found only in humble homes. That peace was guaranteed by the fact that so many ordinary men and women, in England as in Europe, desired it was a favourite theme in the public speeches of eminent men, and the conviction had been clearly enunciated as early as 1929 by a writer[1] whose words carried all the more weight as they were detached from any kind of political partisanship. But the promoters of the Ballot were anxious to achieve something higher than mere optimism about the future. They believed that not only would the Ballot be 'educative' at home, but that abroad it would dispel doubts about England's sincerity for the causes of Peace and the League—doubts due to our ancient reputation for hypocrisy and humbug; and in this way much-needed assurance and direction would be given to a Europe anxious to have a lead from us. Another highly moral object lesson for foreigners. In this object the Ballot undoubtedly succeeded. The Dictators concluded that, so far as England was concerned, they could go ahead.

---

[1] ' After all, if Great Britain and the U.S.A., France, Germany, Italy and Japan say that there shall be no more war, war will certainly not happen on the great scale.' (Dr. Cyril Norwood, *The English Tradition in Education*, p. 291.)

This incident has been analysed at some length in order to reveal the dangers inherent in certain causes with which Fisher was honourably and sincerely associated. He was an idealist member of an idealist political party, and in common with many contemporaries he was induced to give public support to a movement which assumed that these ideals, so much valued by ourselves, can be shipped across the Channel. That the Channel divides us from a different mentality is an assertion which would find greater credence now than it would have done ten years ago, and Fisher himself had an opportunity in May, 1934, of gauging this difference, not only of mentality, but of moral sense. The occasion was an interesting discussion in his lodgings with the Duke and Duchess of Brunswick. In the course of the discussion the Warden maintained that young Englishmen wanted bygones to be bygones, and that Germany should try to become reconciled to British youth. He was shocked by German persecution of the Jews. To this the Duchess (daughter of the ex-Kaiser) replied that after the war the Jews had got the upper hand, and ruling families had been dethroned. King Alfonso had been ejected from Spain, and there had been no protest about that. Fisher, perhaps unable to contend with this somewhat oblique line of argument, deplored the penalising of Jewish intellectuals and attacks on the independence of universities, citing Einstein as an instance; to which Her Grace replied somewhat cryptically that ' Einstein meddled in politics.' The conversation then turned to disarmament, and the Duchess expressed the opinion that, if Germany disarmed, then she was entitled to a good ' quid pro quo.' The apparently innocent Latin tag concealed a world of meaning, of which the Duchess herself may have been quite unaware. When a man promises to put down his loaded pistol if we make it worth his while, we regard the transaction as criminal; but the same procedure, on an infinitely larger scale, appeared to the Duchess, as to millions of virtuous and devout Germans, no more than a piece of sound policy. Those who would ' re-educate ' Germany will have to deal not only with the habits of bad Germans, but (a far more difficult task) with the thoughts of the good ones.

Fisher's activities in the last decade of his life would have been sufficient to provide for three well-occupied men. The labour of completing his *History of Europe*, combined as it was with so many other exacting duties, led to a slight stroke in the later part of 1935. He made a wonderful recovery, and by the spring of 1936 he was sufficiently restored to go for his convalescence to the south of Spain. The illness left a slight suggestion of fragility, but otherwise his mind was as clear and his energy as undiminished as ever. He had not abandoned his hope that Europe would remain at peace, for right up to the Munich incident of 1938 he hoped that Germany, in some way or other, would become ' de-Hitlerised ', and he deplored the outcry against the Munich ' settlement '. But by the spring of 1939 he had come to dread the worst. The Government was now acting on the assumption that hostilities were likely to ensue, and in June Fisher accepted the chairmanship of the Appellate Tribunal for Conscientious Objectors, a capacity in which he gave his last service to the State. It was a tribute to his humanity and sense of justice that he was given such a post, and it may have been known that as a Cabinet Minister in the war of 1914–8 he had opposed the ' cat and mouse ' method of releasing conscientious objectors after serving a sentence only to send them back to imprisonment; nor had he given any countenance to the demands, made by men few of whom had ever heard a shot fired in earnest and many of whom had profited financially by the war, that conscientious objectors should be disfranchised and debarred from earning a living in the teaching profession. Fisher was not himself in sympathy with the reasons, whether religious or political, which have been urged to justify a pacifist attitude in war, and he knew that often these reasons were mere pretexts; but on the other hand he recognised the fact, as many of his contemporaries failed to realise it, that the Act rightly or wrongly gave exemption to those who could give clear evidence of a conscientious objection to participation in war. ' A belief,' he wrote, ' for which a man is willing to suffer imprisonment, contumely and ruin has all the qualities attaching to a religious creed ';[1] within the category of ' conscientious objector ' were to be found some of the best as well as some of the meanest of mankind. It could not be expected that the local tribunals would be able to distinguish between the two, and their jurisdiction, conducted mainly by elderly and indignant men assisted by lawyers in uniform, often defied the most elementary principles of English justice,

[1] Fisher, *The Commonweal*, p. 129.

usually by assuming the guilt, that is, the insincerity of the appellant before he could state his case. Indeed, these tribunals purported to determine on something which is notoriously beyond the scope of a law court, namely, a man's conscience, and inevitably this jurisdiction was so full of vagaries and inconsistencies as to justify in some measure foreign opinion about English sincerity. Thus, in the later months of 1939 while the South-Western tribunal gave 41 per cent. of total exemptions, London gave only 4 per cent., and in the same period while the Midlands gave 74 per cent. conditional exemptions and only 7 per cent. non-combatant, the North-Eastern tribunal gave these exemptions in almost equal proportions. Eleven of these local tribunals were established, appeals from which were to be held by the Appellate Tribunal, which also could hear cases of men who, claiming a conscientious objection, had served a sentence of three months or more for refusing military duty. The higher tribunal was given power to take evidence on oath, and the appellant might have the assistance of counsel or of a friend. With his two colleagues, Sir Leonard Costello, a retired Indian judge, and Sir Arthur Pugh, ex-chairman of the T.U.C., Fisher began his duties in December, 1939, his intention being to do as much as possible of the work in vacation, and to travel to London in term-time on not more than two days a week.

From the start he made clear his view that exemption could not be claimed on political grounds (in spite of the Bristol tribunal's acceptance of these), but only on religious or moral grounds. He urged on the Ministry of Labour special consideration of a type of case not explicitly covered by the Act—that of the son of a shell-shocked parent who could give evidence of nervous condition due to his father's disability. On this point the help of Lord Horder was invited, and it may be said generally that in the war of 1939–45 the attitude to such cases has been both more humane and more scientific than that which prevailed in 1914–18, when nervous failure was usually regarded as cowardice. Fisher also advocated that those who were willing to serve in the R.A.M.C. should be allowed to do so, and that there should be an enlargement of the range of occupations to which conscientious objectors might be posted. In this connection he mentioned minesweeping as an alternative for the man who objected to the taking of human life, thus showing that he shared the popular misconceptions about minesweeping. Closer experience of war conditions would have enabled him to realise that minesweeping is not necessarily a pacifist occupation, because the minesweepers had often to defend themselves, usually against heavy odds, and moreover the minesweepers would have indignantly resented the idea that their service should be a dumping-ground for conscientious objectors.

Proceedings began early in December, 1939, the first case being that of a youth who had given up an engineering job when he found that he was making torpedo parts. He was willing to accept non-combatant service, and as evidence of his conscientious objection he cited his membership of a sect named the Exclusive Brethren. The Tribunal had never heard of this sect and dismissed the appeal. A member of the Methodist Peace Fellowship appealing against non-combatant work under Army control met with the same fate. Unconditional exemption was refused to a Welsh Sunday-school teacher and a Post Office worker. Among the questions asked by the Tribunal were: 'What sacrifices have you made?' and 'Are you a teetotaller?', questions which illustrate the difficulty, some would say the absurdity, of trying to determine what is in a man's mind. But if Fisher could do little to improve a judicature capable at best of only a haphazard equity, he at least strove to instil into the Appellate Tribunal a spirit of humanity, and his efforts in this direction were warmly appreciated both by his colleagues and by the Government. When, in January, 1940, the number of appeals rose to a hundred per week, he realised that two days' attendance during the weeks of term-time were insufficient, and accordingly he intimated that his resignation would take effect the following April.

Fisher was now in his seventy-fifth year, having completed the five years' extension of his Wardenship granted by a special resolution of the College. It was now proposed to extend his tenure for another period, a measure which could be effected only by the consent of the Visitor, the Bishop of Winchester, on the petition of a majority of the Fellows. The petition for this purpose was unanimous, and in January, 1940, the Visitor, Dr. Cyril Garbett, gladly gave his approval to the extension. This testimony of unimpaired powers and of continued appreciation by those who knew him best gave great pleasure to the Warden, whose knowledge and judgment were of special value to the College in the difficulties created by the war; indeed, his calmness and quiet confidence at this time were a source of strength to all with whom he came into contact. At Easter, in the company of the Visitor he inspected the now completed New Library, and he resumed his attendances at the conscientious objectors' tribunal in London, intending that these should be concluded at the end of the month. It was while on his way to the tribunal that he was knocked down by a motor vehicle, and though he rallied to such an extent that for a few days recovery seemed possible, his injuries proved fatal, and he died in St. Thomas's Hospital on April 18, 1940. His ashes were placed in the cloisters of New College, where an inscription in Latin records his services to learning, to education and to the state.

VIII

Fisher as Writer

FISHER, like most classical scholars, had a keen appreciation of literary style. He devoted much time and labour to the perfecting of his prose until it became a flexible, nervous instrument for the expression of his thought, its careful modulation helping to bring into relief the epigrams which were distributed at judicious intervals. Such cultivation of literary style is now rare among historians, who are usually suspicious of exposition which reveals conscious effort; by contrast Fisher, who always considered his public, tried to write in such a manner that his readers would be tempted to read right to the end, and so, unlike some of his contemporaries, he need never be taken for granted, not always an advantage in critical circles. It is true that occasionally Fisher's writing is lacking in effectiveness; sometimes the phrasing is conventional, or the adjectives too numerous; more usually his English has the apparently effortless flow which conceals much hard work. Style, however, is something more than mere mechanism of sentence and paragraph. It is the result of a process of thought, of an attempt to arrive at a complete understanding of the subject in order that its exposition may be easily comprehended, a process necessitating intelligent selection, and so not available for those who can leave nothing out. Fisher's prose style was good in the sense that it was the clear expression of what was worth saying.

Omitting his *History of Europe*, which is the subject of a separate chapter, Fisher's historical work falls into two distinct classes, one the product of research on subjects chosen by himself, the other the fulfilment of a commission, whether resulting from a lecture engagement or from inclusion in a series. In the first class are *The Mediæval Empire* (1898) and *Napoleonic Statesmanship, Germany* (1903), the former a disappointment, because the subject demanded more time and thought than he was able to devote to it,

the latter a success, because the theme, though still vast, was more
clearly defined, and there was a better proportion between the time
devoted to research and that devoted to the writing of the book.
Much of the interest of *Napoleonic Statesmanship* is due to a
paradox, or at least a contrast, so well maintained that it provides
a keynote—the contrast between the high-sounding principles of
Napoleonic statecraft and the exploitation of countries subjected
to these principles. On the one hand were professions of enlightenment, of progress, of ruthless extirpation of the old sloth and
obscurantism; on the other hand, the application of these principles
meant for Germany ' an army of spies and custom-house officers, of
insolent soldiers and corrupt officials, of extortion, repression and
despotism.'[1] It was the kind of antithesis which Fisher loved to
handle, and he did it with a wealth of illustration which made vivid
what otherwise might have been merely laborious and dull; moreover, the readableness of the book helps to obscure the fact that it
was the result of prolonged investigation mainly in provincial
German archives. A monograph on a worth-while subject, it has a
creative element rare in such books. Here, and perhaps here only,
did Fisher do full justice to the influence of F. W. Maitland.

Napoleonic Statesmanship reveals another of Fisher's good
qualities—his ability to produce little pen portraits, not unworthy
of those among his ancestors who were amateur artists of distinction.
Here, for example, is a description of Hanover.[2]

' Imagine a flat and sandy waste, here and there relieved by
tracts of thriving forest and arable land, and only on its southern
boundary by rolling, pine-clad hills; with a few small towns, the
largest, Hanover, containing but 16,500 souls, with little trade or
commerce; with no political journals; its roads bad; its villages
collections of miserable huts; its peasantry, save in the Elbe
marches and in Hadeln, subject to onerous feudal services; its
politicians all aristocrats supported by Court offices, and therefore
timorous and dependent; its towns governed by narrow and
domineering oligarchies; its university learned, but obsequious;
its industries stifled by guilds and uninformed by mechanical or
chemical knowledge; its government, local and central, a chaos
of disparate and independent institutions grown together by

---

[1] *Napoleonic Statesmanship, Germany,* p. 349.   [2] *Ibid.,* p. 51.

accident and the lapse of time; its law antique, barbarous, chaotic —such was the Electorate of Hanover, a country inhabited by a population more insular than the English, and long sunk in the lethargy which is the product of a bad political and social constitution, of consistent neglect, and of the absence of large national hopes.'

And this is Hamburg:[1]

' Though the streets were unlighted and unpaved, the feasts of the merchant princes were worthy of Lucullus. It was currently said that you should breakfast in Scotland, sup in France, but dine in Hamburg, and the visitor who gazes upon the loaded barges, the grim warehouses and the dark and tortuous canals of this northern Venice may feel that Lessing's onslaught on the classical canons of French dramatic art is not inappropriate to the Teutonic genius of the place.'

It is a curious and even disturbing fact that of all Fisher's historical writings these were the only two that can be described as completely spontaneous, in the sense that both subject and scope of treatment were entirely his own; it may even have been the success of his *Napoleonic Statesmanship, Germany* which prevented his continuing to write such books. At first he had thought of writing a similar volume for Napoleonic administration in Italy, but in view of the time and expense which the investigation of Italian archives would have entailed, the proposal had to be abandoned, and meanwhile he was being pressed to contribute books to series or give lecture courses, for all of which there was the attraction of immediate recompense, and avoidance of the commercial risk involved by publication of an independent work of learning. Had his repute been less, he would not have been offered so many commissions, and so would have had more time on his hands; he was now able to publish without financial risk, but only at the cost of a certain amount of independence. An example is his volume on the period 1485–1558 which he contributed in 1906 to Longmans' well-known series *The Political History of England*, where he was obliged to adhere to the editorial conception of what ' political history ' connoted. Like all Fisher's work, the book is well written and readable, but like the other volumes in the series it seldom goes very far below the surface, and is more a narrative of events than a history of England during the Reformation, with the result that we are told very little about those social and economic changes which laid the foundations of modern England. Of these books 'made to order' a better example is his short biography of Napoleon published in 1913 as a volume in the Home University Library. It is probably the best short account of Napoleon's career, and it is a striking example of how good a short book can be; one would like to describe it as brilliant, but for the fact that this term has been ruined by over-use.

In the same category are the published lectures, notably *The Republican Tradition in Europe* (the Lowell lectures delivered in Boston in 1912), and *Bonapartism*, a series of lectures delivered in University College, London, in 1907. The former, which covers a wide field, is eloquent and judicious, abounding in epigrams and sound generalisations, but occasionally slight in both substance and thought; in parts it recalls the good text-book rather than a serious contribution to the subject. For this the level of Fisher's audience may have been partly responsible. *Bonapartism*, though still of a semi-popular character, is on a somewhat higher plane. As his audience was probably more critical, and as the subject related to the ever-congenial Napoleon, Fisher was able to give much better evidence of his quality. He knew France and the Napoleonic era better perhaps than any English contemporary, and he had the philosopher's grasp of the principles underlying the many contacts and reactions of the French Revolution. It is for this reason that these lectures are of special interest to the student of contemporary politics, for they elucidate some of the elements which may be expected in all revolutions. Thus, Fouché, the brutal Chief of Police, has had a recent counterpart; then as now acquiescence might be won by fear of a worse alternative—'so long as the Napoleonic regime lasted, bourgeois and peasant felt themselves sheltered from the quadruple menace of socialists, royalists, clericals and Jews ';[1] the lie, constantly reiterated, had the same effectiveness—'the Emperor who cheated at cards had no scruple in suppressing or falsifying facts. . . . On a scale unprecedented in history he erected

[1] *Bonapartism*, p. 39.

mendacity into an art of empire.'[1] Most striking of all is the restlessness of the dictators, for behind their catch-phrases they never know what they really want—'There was never so restless a diplomatist [as Napoleon]. He would change the boundaries of states and open up new horizons from month to month, like a child who amuses itself with bricks . . . feeling that nothing was intended to last.'[2] Supermen and revolutionaries captivate contemporaries by an appearance of novelty, but they run monotonously true to form.

This philosophic interest can be found elsewhere in Fisher's approach to history, notably in his Creighton Lecture *Political Unions* (1911). Inspired mainly by the recent Union of South Africa, this lecture sought to determine the circumstances which appear to favour a successful union or federation. Federation assumes a partition of sovereignty, and in South Africa neither the native problem nor the railway problem could be divided; moreover, in the coast colonies there was a feeling of patriotic forbearance which led them to make sacrifices for the sake of the greater efficiency secured by a union. From this starting-point the lecturer tried to discover the reasons why some unions had been so short-lived—for example, those of Holland and Belgium, Norway and Sweden, Spain and Portugal. These examples illustrate the difficulty of fusing together two communities each of which has a strong national consciousness, and Fisher was tempted to conclude that in such cases two is an unfortunate number, since a dualism becomes inevitable, and the forces of separatism are then at their maximum. The exception is the union of England and Scotland, for the success of which there was this, among other special reasons, that the Scots were willing to surrender their Parliament provided they retained their Church; moreover, the two partners had each a greater sense of restraint or tolerance than is usually found among continental peoples. Where the number of contracting parties is greater than two, antagonisms may be neutralised—'the more complex the interplay of material, religious and political factors, the more easy it is to maintain a stable combination.' This is true of the United States, where the union has been seriously threatened only once, and then by the accident that the slavery-freedom question created a dualism. So too in Germany, where the numerous political parties overflow and obscure

---

[1] *Ibid.*, p. 51.   [2] *Ibid.*, p. 53.

the old state boundaries. Fisher emphasised how unity might be fostered by things not obviously political in character, for example a railway; Canada he quoted as an example of ' a nation strung upon a thread of steel.' The lecture concluded with the observation that political unions have made a great contribution to the cause of peace and civilisation, as most clearly evidenced by the greatest of all unions, that of nations within the British Empire.

In his Raleigh Lecture *The Whig Historians*, delivered in 1928 when he was President of the British Academy, Fisher gave some indication of his own political and historical loyalties, and put up a good defence of the most maligned of all historians—Macaulay. He alluded to the deep-seated tradition that a readable historian must necessarily be unreliable, and that conversely all dull historians are sound. With our complete detachment from patriotic bias we condemn Macaulay as a liar, or at best a romancer, while in Ranke and other German historians we find the highest expression of scientific accuracy and truth. But in this lecture Fisher was concerned not so much with our academic preference for Teutonic historiography, as with the popular disparagement of Macaulay, and the increasing emphasis laid on the value of those histories which avowedly state a case in favour of some party other than the Whig party, or seek to rehabilitate those persons, usually Stuart rulers or their ministers, whom the Whigs have disparaged, or are presumed to have disparaged. The great Whig historians, concerned mainly with the development of toleration and our parliamentary institutions, may often in a spirit of complacency have ignored other important elements in national life, and Fisher was ungrudging in his recognition of the value which such alternative interpretations may have. But nevertheless he was convinced that English political institutions, including our freedom of discussion, owed more to the Whigs than to the Tories, and that so long as we are a middle-class democracy the Whig historian is likely to be more representative than the Tory or Radical, who usually can speak only on behalf of minorities or extremes. Nor had he any sympathy with those who sneer at ' the mother of parliaments ' which, after all, has survived so many more colourful rivals.

Of Macaulay, Fisher had some cogent things to say. We all admit that he is readable, but few are aware of the immense labours in original sources which underlay his narrative. Macaulay, it is true, had less experience of foreign diplomatic archives than had Ranke, but then he did not regard foreign policy as the sole or even the main object of his enquiry, for he assumed that the history of a nation is as wide and varied as its life. He created a living thing, the imperfections of which are obvious; they would have been less obvious had he given us only a skeleton or a physiological section. His political bias is public and unashamed; to that extent we are less likely to be misled by him than by those historians who insist on their own impartiality. A man of immense learning, he had two qualities not always associated with erudition—namely, intense conviction in certain great causes, and a powerful imagination which enabled him to visualise what he was describing; in this way he was the antithesis of that type of historian who achieves some kind of formal accuracy by limiting the perspective, omitting the controversial, and hedging every conclusion with so many reservations that the reader is left with no impression other than that of the 'caution' of the writer. Temperamentally, Fisher had none of the robustness of Macaulay, but they had one thing in common—they were prepared, as historians, to take risks. They were builders rather than members of demolition squads, and after all a building is usually of more value than a heap of rubble. There were other things in common between the two men. Like Macaulay, Fisher had had 'a direct share in public life, or access to the society of governing people,' and so both could claim personal experience of many of those problems which under different guises are recurrent in history. Still more, Fisher's interpretation of history, like that of Macaulay, was not limited by the standards of the reviewer, or by the requirements of some specialist or exclusive school of research, but was an essential part of his Liberalism, in which he believed as intensely as had Macaulay in his Whig principles, and so embodies his outlook on life.

His interest in men who shared this outlook led him to write three biographies. The largest of these was that devoted to James Bryce (two volumes, 1927). He was one of Bryce's executors, and there were points of strong contrast and resemblance between the two. They were contrasted most obviously in their antecedents: the one a product of Scottish-Ulster stock, a dour, hard-headed, but usually warm-hearted race; the other representative of the more polished and metropolitan atmosphere of southern, Anglican England. Bryce was by profession an academic jurist; he was politically ineffective because he always saw both sides of a question; he had few social graces, though he had many devoted friends; Fisher, on the other hand, had an eye for his public, he was a consummate diplomatist, and he was a social success. But they shared certain things of temperament and circumstance. Both had a singularly happy home life. They were devoted to ideals of enlightenment and toleration, and they each consecrated a long and busy life to the cause of these ideals. As Gladstonian Liberals they were survivals, each in his generation subjected to an accelerating process of disillusionment. Each of them is remembered for a great book.

Fisher's biography is a good piece of literary workmanship, but no more. To the end Bryce remains somewhat remote, his career unrelieved by failing or failure, nor does the author succeed in connecting the writer with the statesman. Two volumes are made to do the work of one. The moral is perhaps that a biographer should select for a subject a person of entirely different career and temperament, for in such conditions a better sense of proportion may be achieved, and the delineation may be more convincing, as witness George Otto Trevelyan's *Early Life of C. J. Fox* or J. W. Mackail's *William Morris*, or David Cecil's *The Stricken Deer*, to name only three of the best biographies in our language. A reading of Fisher's *Bryce* recalls not a living personality but an adequate description of a figure in a pantheon.

The accounts of F. W. Maitland and Paul Vinogradoff are so much shorter that they may be described as Memoirs. In Maitland, Fisher was fortunate enough to have a subject many of whose letters are worth quoting *in extenso*—a tremendous asset to a biographer—and these letters reveal something of the personal charm of the brother-in-law. The book is an eloquent and graceful tribute to one whom Fisher regarded with admiration and affection; moreover, full justice is done to the modesty, the whimsicality and the sense of humour which distinguished the Downing Professor among his academic contemporaries. Another service to the memory of Maitland was Fisher's edition in three volumes of his brother-in-law's unpublished writings,[1] and in 1908 he published what is now Maitland's best-known work, the *Constitutional History of England*, originally a series of lectures given to a small audience, now the joy of the more intelligent student of English history, and the despair of all who prefer strictly-enunciated dogma. It was probably Maitland's co-operation with Paul Vinogradoff (1854–1925) which started Fisher's interest in the Russian scholar, an interest which ripened into friendship when, as Warden of New College, Fisher had occasion to see more of his old friend the Corpus Professor of Jurisprudence. The two men shared an intolerance of mediocrity; neither was fully accepted by the academic world, for Vinogradoff's published work was thought by some to be heavy and turgid, while Fisher's output was considered guilty, on occasion, of the other extreme; both were natural-born teachers, leaving no successors, but providing a stimulus to two generations of students. Still more, Fisher was attracted to the Russian by the fact that he had sacrificed a lucrative position in his native country in order to maintain his intellectual freedom, and so the memoir *Paul Vinogradoff* (1927) is not only a well-informed and well-written account of the career of a great jurist and historian, but is a tribute to the cause of liberty which, by his sacrifice, Vinogradoff had vindicated.[2]

A wider public was reached in *The Commonweal* (1924), the published version of the Stevenson Lectures on Citizenship delivered in the preceding year in the University of Glasgow. Here we have a glimpse of Fisher's philosophy of life, a philosophy based on the idea of the responsibility of the individual to the State. He thought that there was nothing anti-social in the possession of great wealth ' honestly acquired '; what was anti-social was the abuse of such wealth. He deplored the fact that class suspicion had been developed to such an extent that even the noblest uses of money were often decried. Material success in life might easily in his opinion be combined with the pursuit of high ideals, for the capitalist system need not necessarily be selfish. Class distinction is easily exaggerated, and it is often forgotten that the advantages obtained by one section of society (e.g. by the barons of Magna Carta) may ultimately become

[1] *Collected Papers of F. W. Maitland* (1911).
[2] In 1928 Fisher edited, in two volumes, the *Collected Papers of Paul Vinogradoff*.

the rights and privileges of a nation. Civilisation as we know it in Europe had, he maintained, been built up on the foundation of private property; the defects of an institution are no proper justification for its abolition, and our real dangers, in his opinion, were to be found not in our inequitable distribution of property, but in the forces of ignorance and bigotry which exist independently of any economic considerations. Hence he deplored the current attitude to writers such as Lucian, Voltaire and Anatole France, who are usually dismissed as evil-minded cynics. 'What is deepest in these three great men-of-letters,' declared the lecturer, 'is a serious and all-pervading concern for the high claims of human reason, a belief in good sense and tolerance and clemency, coupled with a detestation of the cruelty, the fanaticism and the superstition which debase human nature.'[1] The warning was timely. In our concern for only the economic factors in civilisation we may ignore those finer elements essential not only to the good life of the individual but to the well-being of the State. 'We do not measure nations only by the volume of their trade—we judge them by the quality of their civilisation.'[2]

The Stevenson lectures show an appreciation of education as something social rather than personal. 'In general, the wider a man's education, the richer and more varied his equipment of ideas, the greater the span of his interests, the more valuable will he be to his fellows.'[3] He was obviously distinguishing between education and book-learning, and he admitted that even the most elaborate system of state education cannot produce wisdom; indeed, he went so far as to recognise a social danger in the unlimited extension of educational facilities, since a rise in society by means of the educational ladder is usually followed by a sterilising process, 'which everywhere follows upon social success.' In other words, in proportion as they become educated the poor will have smaller families, and a community in which all are educated would probably become extinct in a few generations. Moreover, according to Fisher, poverty has its eugenic value, as it tends to eliminate the stocks 'which are unequal to the burden of modern civilisation.'[4] Such doctrines come strangely from the author of the Bill of 1918. He was speaking,

---

[1] *The Commonweal*, p. 54.
[2] *Ibid.*, p. 30.
[3] *Ibid.*, p. 50.
[4] *Ibid.*, p. 148.

however, not on a popular platform, but before a university audience, and hence these may be regarded as his real convictions. Throughout, he appeared sometimes as an Aristotelian, more often as a Platonist, seldom as a Liberal, and never as a politician.

Inevitably, the lectures allude to the increasing international tension. ' The real malady of Europe,' he declared, ' is not economic, but moral and political.'[1] New hatreds and old feuds were corrupting the life-blood of Europe, all of them disguised under some economic catchword. Here Fisher was probably right, where so many others certainly were wrong. He thought that one of the most necessary requirements for tranquillising the Continent was the discovery of some means of allaying the apprehensions of France, and he mentioned that ' to meet the special needs of France, the League has been considering the scheme of an open treaty of mutual guarantee to come into effect *as soon as the nations concerned have carried out an agreed plan of disarmament.*'[2] The italicised words suggest that Fisher, so perspicacious in judging the real causes of European unrest, was content to find a remedy in the jargon of Geneva.

Fisher was on surer ground when he claimed that beauty is an essential element in social welfare. ' One great building reclaims a wilderness of squalor. The artistic reputation of a town has been founded on an organ, a church, a single old master.'[3] The Stevenson lecturer probably did not realise how cogently this statement might have been illustrated from the city in which he was speaking, for within a few yards of him, in a municipal art gallery which houses many masterpieces, was the original of Rembrandt's *Man in Armour*, and within two miles of his lecture hall was a mediaeval cathedral, saved from the vandalism of sixteenth-century Reformers by the spirited defence of the Glasgow apprentices. But a lecturer on Citizenship is not expected to know anything of the traditions of the city where he is speaking; his remarks, equally valid for Sheffield or Bournemouth, usually have a detachment from those local things which may mean so much to the inhabitants, and this may be the reason why the subject of Civics (if it can be called a subject) has been found so insipid by many enquirers. There are few towns in Great Britain which cannot boast something in which the citizens

---

[1] *Ibid.*, p. 18.   [2] *Ibid.*, p. 247.   [3] *Ibid.*, pp. 90–91.

can take pride, and this human, personal element is often the starting-point of a wider interest in public affairs. It is an unfortunate thing that many of these traditions have been obscured by industrial development, or by alien immigration, and from these two causes Glasgow, with its long and varied history, has suffered more than any other city in Europe. Fisher, always sensitive to these things, probably concluded that they were outside the terms of his lectureship.

A still wider but not always appreciative public was reached by *Our New Religion*, which first appeared in 1929. The book stands quite apart from Fisher's other writings, and it is not clear why he wrote it. His visits to the United States may have impressed him with a sense of how Christian Science had captured America, or he may have witnessed its potentialities for good and evil in the example of a relative. What is certain is that he experienced much mortification from the reception of this book. He was as disappointed with the sales as with the reviews; the book was banned by some of the most influential book-selling agencies in America, and he had to write several letters repudiating the insinuation, assiduously spread, that he had apologised for the book and had withdrawn it. All this provided the only occasion on which he came near to what he dreaded most—notoriety. It is a singular comment on one of the most advanced of modern civilisations that a book so harmless as this should have evoked not so much denunciation as ostracism, and to the outsider it must appear that a movement so sensitive to criticism must have something to conceal. *Our New Religion* is the best-written of all Fisher's books, and one of the finest pieces of English which this century has yet produced.

This little book suggests an era different from that in which we live. Satire is dead, not because there are no satirists, but because we instinctively turn away from anything which threatens to undermine our delicately-poised conventions; we dislike throwing stones because so many of us have to live in glass houses, and as civilisation progresses men are obliged to recognise that the line dividing honesty from its converse becomes more difficult to determine. Truth, the most corrosive of all the virtues, might well play havoc with the well-oiled machinery of modern society. These considerations may help to explain why *Our New Religion* was received with such hostility in certain influential quarters. But Fisher had not written the book in any spirit of sarcasm; he had, it is true, a liking for *jeux d'esprit*, and in intimate circles he often showed a spirit of irresponsible gaiety, qualities which are faintly discernible in this book; but though he could not for long have maintained the rôle of a Pope or a Dryden he occasionally experienced something of the moral indignation of a Juvenal. Beneath the irony of the book few critics detected its serious purpose. That purpose was primarily a social one. In common with other educated men Fisher knew the tremendous value to society of the medical services, and of the men and women who devote their lives to these services. To him it seemed not only preposterous but suicidal that all this should be thrust aside for the mumbo-jumbo of an ignorant old woman, whose profitable incoherences provided the basis of a cult in which religion and commercialism were dexterously combined. 'The dream of Christian Science,' he wrote, 'is that sickness and sin, pain and death are themselves dreams, unreal emanations of an unreal mind, and destined to disappear before the advancing sunlight of faith. What religion has made larger promises to mankind than this? What dreams have been more sanguine or defiant? And what edifice has ever been more vulnerable to the daily thrust of unpleasant fact?'[1]

Fisher would have been the last person to deny the power of faith in the therapeutics of bodily and spiritual ailments; and every wise exponent of the healing art, whether physician or priest, knows that faith will often effect a cure where drugs or dogma will fail. But what Fisher resented most in the Christian Scientists was their claim to be the only accredited faith healers, and their implied assumption that all disorders can be cured by spiritual means. Obviously such claims, if consistently maintained by a community, would result in a dangerously high death rate. But these claims are not pressed to their conclusion, and so, according to Fisher, the movement derives its strength mainly from comfortably-off hypochondriacs, mostly idle women, whose ailments, such as they are, can easily be ministered to by tactful practitioners with a reasonable hope of success; while for more obvious complaints, such as a broken leg, prayer may have to be supplemented by recourse to the ordinary doctor. Where the practice of Christian Science is confined within

[1] *Our New Religion*, p. 119.

these limits it is possible that no great harm is done, for the money so spent might otherwise go to palmists and soothsayers. But who can determine the borderline between the harmless and harmful ailment? Can the Christian Science practitioner always be trusted to know when a doctor should be called in? And must the sick child be denied proper medical treatment merely because the parents are devotees of a particular faith? Fisher had no doubt that an apparently harmless movement might easily become a social menace. But there is really little danger of this, since like so many fashionable cults Christian Science does not penetrate beneath a certain economic and social level.

His suggestion that Christian Science was essentially a disagreeable by-product of American civilisation may partly account for the reception of the book in the United States. Leisure which threatened to become boredom, fortunes acquired by get-rich-quick methods, education built up on lines of least resistance, a Christianity which had become formal and dull, these in his opinion were the conditions which had favoured Mrs. Eddy, and accounted for the resounding success of her hierophants. Christ had founded a religion for the poor and the suffering; here was a religion for the bored and well-to-do, with all the advantages of modern, high-pressure publicity methods.

Fisher was profoundly interested in founders of new faiths: here is his sketch of Mrs. Eddy as she appeared in 1879:

'Here [in Boston] Mrs. Eddy, now the Reverend Mother, a graceful figure tastefully dressed in black silk, her chestnut hair not yet tinted against the advance of age, her eyes of the deepest blue (or were they grey?), but shielded with spectacles, since "she bore the vices of the world," her voice clear and musical, would lecture to large audiences, always confident, always serene, always resounding in sonorous biblical phraseology, and creating upon her listeners that impression of "poise" which in the sharp tingling New England air is so much valued as a sedative for jangled nerves and the uneasy conscience.'

This sketch is delicately drawn, but the artist was engaged on a dangerous commission, because most Anglo-Saxons instinctively dislike any suggestion of ridicule in the portrait of a woman, and this one merits careful scrutiny. It may well be that the reference to spectacles was intended as a clever and legitimate thrust, because after all Mrs. Eddy should not have needed such earthly aids to her vision: but what had the colour of her eyes to do with it? There is just the slightest suggestion of sarcasm in his question whether the colour was blue or grey, and it may well be that touches like this have given offence, and understandable offence. In one other respect Fisher was somewhat unfair to Christian Scientists, when he objected that their practitioners accepted fees. Now such an objection is entirely beside the point; if it is upheld, it might be levelled against almost any form of professional remuneration, including the fees derived by Fisher himself from his lectures in the United States, where he was nearly as popular with his audiences as the Reverend Mother had been. We all appreciate condemnations of knavery; it is when we descend to particulars, especially where a woman is concerned, that we have to be most careful. *Our New Religion* ought to have been written in French with all the personal names left out.

The last of Fisher's miscellaneous writings which call for brief notice here is the *Unfinished Autobiography*, published posthumously in 1940. This personal record was begun shortly after the outbreak of war in 1939, and the narrative is carried down to about 1924. It is specially valuable and informative for his early years, and contains the only record of his experiences as a student in Paris and Germany; the book also reveals his enthusiasm for education and his triumph over the difficulties besetting the Act of 1918. The author's sense of proportion saved him from burdening the record with the irrelevant, his concern being mainly with matters of interest or importance, and so he seldom indulges in the tittle-tattle so often found in writings of this kind. Also, it should be remembered that the book is no more than an unrevised fragment of what might otherwise have been a concerted work. In recent years many distinguished men have anticipated their future biographers by publishing their autobiographies, supplying contemporaries with much useful information, but occasionally embarrassing posterity by saying things which might more appropriately come from other pens. In cannot be pretended that Fisher's *Autobiography* is altogether free from this characteristic. But a good autobiography

FISHER AS WRITER

is a very rare thing; nor is its success necessarily commensurate with the successes enjoyed by the author, for we instinctively feel that real achievement is often preceded or accompanied by much of that misfortune and frustration which many of us have known in our own obscure lives. The absence of obvious failure in Fisher's career made his autobiography an even more difficult task than his biography. But he will not be remembered by his own account of the things which brought him temporary fame, for it was in the contemplation and delineation of the great past, a laborious and saddening discipline, that he attained not only a surer standard of values, but a richer humanity and even, most precious of all, a sense of humility, the qualities which will ensure for his *History of Europe* a more permanent place in the esteem of mankind.

IX

The History of Europe

THE inception of this book may be found in a letter written by
Douglas Jerrold to Fisher in June, 1926, where the writer stated that
he had been inspired by his reading of H. G. Wells's *Outline of
History* to plan a full-scale history of the world. Jerrold, convinced
that Wells's history was 'tendentious,' and that the *Cambridge
Modern History* provided no more than the materials for history,
suggested a consecutive account for the educated man in fifteen to
twenty volumes, with full references, but with 'a wholesale omission
of detail.' The proposed work should, in his opinion, 'bear the
impression of a single mind, written by a man of very liberal understanding, trained in the exact and scholarly use of available materials
—a history of the working out of cause and effect rather than a
narrative of events.' Fisher was asked to undertake this project,
either personally, or as editor, since 'nothing in the way of history
can come out of a committee.' The book was to be called 'The
Oxford History of the World.' But it was not found possible to
proceed on such ambitious lines, and fortunately the work was
ultimately planned to consist of three volumes (one volume in the
popular edition), with Fisher as sole writer. The fulfilment of the
scheme owes much to the vision and energy of Jerrold, an old pupil
of Fisher's, who was acting on behalf of the publishing firm of
Messrs. Eyre and Spottiswoode.

The contract was signed in March, 1931, and specified that the
book should be 'in the nature of a survey, and in no sense a text-
book, although planned to meet not only the requirements of the
general public, but of the upper forms of schools and universities.'
The three volumes were to be entitled 'Mediæval System,' 'Dynamic
Nationalism' and 'Democratic Nationalism,' titles afterwards
changed to 'Ancient and Mediæval' (Vol. I), 'Renaissance, Reformation, Reason' (Vol. II) and 'The Liberal Experiment' (Vol. III).

The first volume was published early in 1935, and the others followed later in the same year, with a dedication to his wife. An unabridged edition in one volume was published by Messrs. Arnold in 1936. New editions have been printed, and many errors were corrected; there were soon proposals for translation into foreign languages, including Hungarian, Polish, Italian, Hebrew and Czech,[1] and there was talk of a German translation, but nothing came of it at the time. From the commercial point of view the enterprise was a success, though the sales in America were disappointing. The five years of intensive work spent on the book, combined with the performance of many other duties, nearly cost the author his life, and it should be recalled that he was sixty-six years of age when he began to write the *History of Europe*. It is one of the very few books which combine the vigour and courage of youth with the judgment and experience of age.

The *History* met with a generous welcome, though some of the signed reviews were tributes not so much to the book as to Fisher's social and academic position, and these were almost fulsome in their eulogy, one such reviewer declaring that 'the whole books calls for nothing but *respectful* cheers.' Of more value were those reviews which pointed out slips or mistakes, of which there were many; there were also more general criticisms, not all of them well founded, but most of them helpful to the author, who always welcomed criticism of his own work and could profit by it. In a different category was the allegation that he had done less than justice to the mediæval Church, an accusation substantiated by nothing more than the selection, from what the author had said about St. Thomas Aquinas, of the phrase 'laborious friar,'[2] with the implication that the great Doctor had been airily dismissed with that epithet, whereas in the preceding sentences Fisher had paid enthusiastic tribute to the genius and influence of Aquinas. Against this type of criticism, which misrepresents by careful omission, there is no defence, for an insinuation once started may have a wide circulation; hence the impression among many Roman Catholics who have not read the book that Fisher was unfair to their Church. The evidence for this

---

[1] The Italian translation, parts of which had to be omitted owing to Fascist censorship, is by Benedetto Croce. There are Hebrew and Hungarian translations. Complete German and Spanish translations are about to be published.

[2] *History of Europe*, p. 283 (the pagination is the same in the three-volume as in the one-volume edition).

is the review above referred to, and the well-known fact that Fisher was an agnostic.

But the author had good reason to be satisfied with the reception of the book, and he soon had evidence that it was being eagerly read far and wide, for it was to be found in the homes of manual workers, in the compartments of railways trains, and in prisoner-of-war camps (where, of course, it was forbidden); indeed, it was read, and read to the last page, by that large and intelligent public which is anxious to know about history, but is naturally shy of historical manuals. An exceptional set of circumstances may account for this unusual fact. One was the boldness of the venture—a one-man history of Europe in an age which entrusted such tasks to committees, an age abounding in historians who have succeeded in demolishing the work of earlier historians, or have written books to show how history ought to be written, or, as often, how it should not be written; another circumstance was the superb skill with which the immense subject was divided up and arranged in natural sequence; a third was the easy and graceful flow of the narrative, often enlivened by an apt allusion, a felicitous epigram, or a penetrating judgment, all maintained at the same comparatively high level, whether the period was the fifth century B.C. or the twentieth century A.D. Throughout, there is that suggestion of effortless ease which conceals infinite labour and thought; the masterpiece of an elaborately-equipped workshop, all the marks of the workshop have been removed.

Every page is stamped with the one original thing in the outfit of the author—his personality, a personality in which an agile intellect was able to draw at will on a vast range of knowledge and experience, or capable of illuminating a subject with the imaginative insight of the artist. Of this latter, the pictorial quality, one example may suffice—the Constantinople erected in the Fourth Century as the new seat of empire: [1]

' The eastern city rose like an exhalation. Palaces and mansions, porticos, law courts and public baths were constructed with feverish celerity. The whole Empire was ransacked for treasures wherewith to decorate the fane of Constantine. While the serpent column reft from Delphi recalled the victory of Plataea, the

[1] *Ibid.*, p. 104.

basilica of the Roman law court crowned with the Persian dome gave to the new Christian churches their characteristic form, a blend of the eastern and the western spirit. On May 11, 330, the work was complete. The new Rome had been built in less than six years.'

Of the former, the allusive quality, many instances appear in the juxtaposition of things not usually associated, a process which often carries conviction once our initial surprise has been overcome; for example this analogy between fifth-century Gaul and nineteenth-century North America:[1]

> 'The cultivated noble of Auvergne feared the defacement of the Latin tongue and the decay of Latin letters. What he did not apprehend was the dissolution of the Latin state. The political consequences of the great changes in the social texture of the population brought about by German immigration was as little present to his mind as were the lessons of American immigration statistics in the last quarter of the nineteenth century to the statesmen in Washington.'

or this, slightly more doubtful or more challenging, between a book produced in sixth-century Byzantium and two others, one of eighteenth-century France and the other of nineteenth-century England:[2]

> 'And so as Western Europe emerged from mediæval darkness it found in the Corpus Juris of Justinian a revelation of the great thing which European civilisation had once been and might again become. The ferment of the mind thus occasioned was immense. Perhaps a faint analogy may be found in the exciting influence at a later stage of human development of Rousseau's *Contrat Social* or Darwin's *Origin of Species*.'

This fertility of illustration, one of Fisher's most distinctive characteristics, is often revealed in a striking or unusual phrase which by the element of surprise helps to hold the attention of the reader; for example, the mediæval Welsh are described as 'a race of quarrelsome nightingales';[3] another is this description of

[1] *Ibid.*, p. 116.   [2] *Ibid.*, p. 134.   [3] *Ibid.*, p. 309.

how the Emperor Justinian chose Theodora to be his Empress:[1] 'he looked into the gutter for a wife and picked out a diamond'; nor could any two sentences be more close-packed than these: 'England grew. Prussia was manufactured.'[2] Only those who bear their learning lightly can write in this way.

All this is evidence not merely of Fisher's learning and literary skill but of his broad humanity, one of the most essential qualities in a historian, but not a universal one. It may be asked whether the absence of definite religious faith limited the extent of that humanity. Any answer to such a question must keep clear two different things, indifference to dogma and indifference to the spiritual element in human life and history. On the first count the author of the *History of Europe* may be indicted, but not on the second, and so far from adopting a materialist view of human conduct, he had a keen appreciation of many of those less tangible factors which may determine the actions of men. The fact that he was for most of his life a keen student and warm admirer of Dante is sufficient evidence that his scepticism involved neither indifference nor hostility to religion. But nevertheless, partly from his agnosticism, partly from his temperament, Fisher was slightly less sensitive than his contemporaries to the good that may be wrought by faith and self-sacrifice; like most historians he was concerned more with obvious achievement than with the strivings and vagaries of those who appear to have failed; as a practical man of affairs he was slightly impatient of the preacher, the mystic, the martyr. Hence in his *History* he finds a place for Bishop Fox the humanist but not for George Fox the Quaker; for St. Francis, but not for St. Theresa; for Lord Shaftesbury, but not for Elizabeth Fry nor for John Howard, and it is not surprising that there is no mention of such 'strays' as Paracelsus, Cagliostro or Spurgeon. Lack of space may well have been the explanation, or the conventional requirements of history-writing, or even his temperament may have helped to dictate the choice. Throughout, the reader of the book is left with the impression of critical acumen rather than of spiritual force.

It is in this critical faculty that Fisher was pre-eminent, and it sometimes appears as a distinctive type of paradox in which certain conventions are implicitly challenged. Thus, most laymen are taught or habituated to connect moral principles with religious doctrines, sanctity with theology and the priesthood with virtue; while, in contrast, immorality and wickedness are more commonly expected of secular men. But in the mind of Fisher, a strictly moral man, detached from all the creeds, this contrast is sometimes given an unexpected twist, not for the pleasure of indulging in mere cleverness, nor from any desire to sneer at sacred things, but possibly in order to suggest an interpretation of life which, piercing through externals, lays bare that confusion of thought which may often dictate the allegiance of masses of men. For so long as men believe ardently in God and the Devil there must arise occasions when these two Powers become confused with or even appear to change places with each other, so that, with equal fervour, good is repudiated for evil, evil is worshipped for good, and whether the cult be of Jehovah or Beelzebub, its leaders are priests, its followers proselytes, and both critics and sceptics are devils to be exterminated. Men, it has been said, are great only when they dream; they are weakest when they have neither faith nor illusions; they are most potent for good or for evil when they worship, because worship is based on conviction, and conviction is the quality which gives men influence over others. Fisher's possible deficiency in ability to appreciate the more remote or more recondite things in human achievement was counterbalanced by his power to penetrate through the most imposing facade of priestly or religious profession, and to reveal that strange mixture of good and evil which, seldom differentiated by the worshippers, may nevertheless determine their acts. It was here, perhaps, that he came nearest to a philosophy of history, or rather to a philosophy of human character and motive as revealed in history. The maxim *corruptio optimi pessima*, if applied to things as well as to persons, helps to suggest what may have been in his mind.

This interpretation, where it occurs, is usually suggested in such a mild and reasonable form as to excite little surprise. Thus, in his analysis of the reasons for the triumph of Roman Christianity, he noted[1] the willingness of Pope Callistus (219–23) to absolve persons guilty of grievous sin, in spite of strong protest against such action. This Fisher regarded as crucial because, in his view, a church may

[1] *Ibid.*, p. 173.

be strengthened by exclusive doctrine, but weakened by exclusive morality. There is therefore an important distinction between things which many regard as identical: 'a church confined in its member-ship to the saints and offering nothing to the sinners would never have effected the conquest of Europe.' There is a similar associa-tion of things usually kept apart in his description of Metternich[1] as 'a man of strict principles and loose morals,' as also in his reference to the Merovingians:[2] 'if the Merovingians were kings, they were also priests. If they were wicked, they were also holy.' Such statements may surprise or even shock some readers, but at least they are neither flippant nor cynical, and may have resulted from a study of human conduct as revealed over long stretches of time.

But everyone admits that the book is fascinating to read. It is just this quality which makes more cogent the question of Fisher's reliability as a historian. We are a conscientious race; some of us read historical romances (in the evening), but none of us will tolerate inaccurate history. Can Mr. Fisher's statements be relied upon? Did he speak the truth? Many readers finish the book with an uneasy feeling that it is too interesting to be true.

Before any attempt can be made to answer this question, it is necessary to refer to some ideals of historiography which have come to be accepted by English scholars, in order to determine with what school of historians Fisher may be classed. The most notable contribution to this subject of historiography has been made by Dr. G. P. Gooch,[3] a historian whose learning and detachment have been warmly admired by every student of the subject, including Fisher himself. Dr. Gooch has paid eloquent tribute to the influence of Ranke, and has shown how the great German historian, breaking fresh ground, set up a standard of history-writing which may be emulated, but rarely rivalled. Ranke was

'the first to divorce the study of the past from the passions of the present, and to relate what actually happened—*wie es eigentlich gewesen*. In his dramas there are neither heroes nor villains. His second service was to establish the necessity of found-ing historical construction on strictly contemporary sources—the

[1] *Ibid.*, p. 929.   [2] *Ibid.*, p. 146.
[3] G. P. Gooch, *History and Historians of the Nineteenth Century*, p. 101.

papers and correspondence of the actors themselves and those in
immediate contact with the events they describe. Thirdly, he
founded the science of evidence by the analysis of authorities,
contemporary or otherwise in the light of the author's temperament . . . and by comparison with the testimony of other writers.
Thenceforth every historian must enquire where his informant
obtained his facts. . . . He was beyond comparison the greatest
historical writer of modern times, and no one has ever approached
so closely to the ideal historian.'[1]

From Ranke dates that 'scientific' school of history which, eliminat-
ing the human factor, derives its information from official documents or material of unimpeachable authenticity and views
humanity with the neutrality of the anatomist. An English
academic historian is valued in proportion as he approaches the
ideals exemplified by Ranke and, to a less extent, by other German
historians. At least two important assumptions are made—first, that
a definite, objective past, history *wie es eigentlich gewesen*, is
knowable; and secondly, that the actual facts and events of that past
are capable of elucidation and expression in a manner which pre-
cludes any element of prejudice or partiality on the part of the
historian.

Ranke is not much read nowadays. He does not deserve this
neglect, for he illuminated vast stretches of history with an
impartiality and learning beyond praise. A Protestant, he wrote a
History of the Popes which can be read with profit and without
offence by the most ardent Roman Catholics; a German, he wrote
a history of England mainly in the seventeenth century which is
still a reliable guide for English readers. But he never claimed to
be 'scientific,' nor would he have denied that, in spite of oneself,
one's interpretation of the past may be coloured by personal factors.
As a German he saw things, as it were, through German spectacles,
and so it was quite natural for him to find in our Magna Carta clear
evidence of 'German personal freedom.'[2] Ranke did his greatest
service by exemplifying the critical handling of materials, but no
more than anyone else did he succeed in narrating history 'as it
had actually happened.'

Second only to Ranke in the names of those who have profoundly

[1] *Ibid.*, p. 101.   [2] Ranke, *History of England,* I, p. 53.

influenced academic historiography in England is Lord Acton, who together with his great predecessor has been taken as the personification of all that is thought best and most characteristic in the Teutonic genius—exalted character, profound learning, high seriousness, untiring industry and unflinching devotion to the truth. More than any other writer Acton impresses by his intense sincerity, a quality which often lends to his statuesque paragraphs a dignity, and on occasion a majesty, such as can be found nowhere else. No historian has ever inculcated such rigorous standards of accuracy and truth. 'There is no palliation of inaccuracy,' he wrote;[1] and in his inaugural lecture as Professor at Cambridge—a lecture hailed as marking the dawn of a new and more scientific age in history writing —he clearly expounded the tenets of his austere creed. Having emphasised how Ranke taught historical study 'to be critical, to be colourless, to be new,'[2] he insisted that our historical judgments must be not only impartial, but based on a high sense of moral responsibility: 'our historical judgments have as much to do with hopes of heaven as public or private conduct.'[3] So too, in his famous Memorandum for the contributors to the *Cambridge Modern History*, he enunciated the strictest standards of what is called 'objectivity':

> 'Contributors will understand that our Waterloo must satisfy French and English, Germans and Dutch alike; that nobody can tell without examining the list of authors where the Bishop of Oxford laid down his pen and whether Fairbairn or Gasquet, Liebermann or Harrison took it up.'

In view of these facts it is not surprising that Acton won the devotion of many enthusiastic admirers, and these may have been in the mind of a singularly well-informed and generous reviewer who wrote thus: 'if an author expresses an opinion different from that of Lord Acton, *so much the worse for the author.*' This statement did not, it is true, succeed in getting into print, but it nevertheless adequately expressed the unavowed principle acted upon by several

[1] Acton, in *Historical Essays and Studies* (1907), p. 384.
[2] *Lecture on the Study of Modern History* (1895), p. 48.
[3] *Ibid.*, p. 20.

earnest-minded and influential men. Acton himself, who had elements of real though occluded greatness in his character, would have been the first to repudiate it, and indeed it was against servility of this kind that he devoted the best energies of his life.

Now it is clear that Fisher scarcely even attempted to achieve any of the high ideals constantly enunciated by Acton and echoed by his followers, ideals usually considered capable if not of fulfil-ment, then of emulation, for they are regarded as the main canons of 'scientific' history. Did Acton practise what he preached? It is necessary to ask and try to answer this question, not in any attempt to discredit the great historian, but in order to justify Fisher and those who believe that the attempt to write history 'as it had actually happened' is both futile and foolish. The fact that Acton did not write very much makes the application of a test more than usually fair, and for this purpose it may be permissible to consider his hand-ling of one of the most curious and obscure incidents in our history —the career of James de la Cloche, or de Cloche, the reputedly eldest of Charles II's natural children. His source of information must first be examined.

Included in Acton's library of nearly 60,000 volumes (all of which he had read at least once) was a biography of Peter Canisius by a Jesuit Father named Giuseppe Boero.[1] Boero published a number of other books, which may have been unknown to Lord Acton, including a biography of the Blessed Peter Favre, the companion of St. Ignatius, which was translated into English in 1873. In this biography[2] Boero records how, when Favre was kneel-ing in the ducal chapel of Gandia before a picture of the Virgin Mary, the eyes of the Virgin were seen to open and to turn lovingly on the suppliant—a miracle witnessed by several persons. The picture, afterwards bequeathed to the Carmelite Convent in Madrid, 'added to the number of miracles' in that sacred institution. But the miracle-working picture of Gandia was easily surpassed by another—that preserved in a Jesuit church at Galloro, a few miles south of Rome, a picture by virtue of which several persons had been restored from death, and many preserved from plague and

[1] *Vita del beato Pietro Canisio*, Rome 1864 (Acton c. b. 144 in Trinity College, Cambridge).
[2] G. Boero, *Life of the Blessed Peter Favre* (English translation, 1873), p. 162.

pestilence. To these extraordinary happenings Father Boero devoted a volume,[1] the success of which may be gauged from the fact that a third edition 'revised and augumented by the author' appeared in 1863. The fact that many of the miracles of Galloro had taken place in the seventeenth century (some of them attested by a notary public) may have intensified the reverend author's interest in a period of history when plots, secrets and visions were the order of the day, and when the partition between this world and the next had appeared, at times, unusually thin. Most interesting of all to the pious chronicler of miracles was the spectacle of our Charles II, at heart a true Catholic, but unwilling to avow it even to himself, and still less to the heretics by whom he was surrounded. But there was a deep secret, still buried in contemporary documents 'of incontestable authenticity' preserved at the Gesù in Rome, of which Boero as librarian had custody. These documents, including five long autograph letters by Charles to the General of the Jesuits, related to the king's eldest son, James de la Cloche, who is supposed to have been born in Jersey about the year 1647. His mother's name is unknown, but it is said that she was of noble rank. James de la Cloche du Bourg de Jersey was therefore senior to the Duke of Monmouth and of much better status on his mother's side.

Charles II is known to have been circumspect in the matter of issuing birth certificates to his numerous progeny, and an elementary acquaintance with the facts of his reign suggests that, when he wished to communicate anything of a specially secret or incriminating character, he preferred to entrust the duty of letter-writing to others, so that his own epistles are always short and discreet. But not so in the secret papers of Father Boero.[2] These contain two

[1] G. Boero, Istoria del santuario della Beatissima Vergine di Galloro (3rd edition, 1863).

[2] The present writer has never seen the originals (preserved at the Gesù in Rome) and is dependent on the Italian translations published by Boero in his Istoria della converzione alla Chiesa Catholica di Carlo II (1863). The Italian versions differ in some important respects from the French originals as quoted by Acton in his Secret History of Charles II (in Acton's Historical Essays and Studies). One of the papers—the Oblatio ex parte Caroli II . . .—is known to readers of Ranke (History of England, III, pp. 393-400), who almost certainly used the copy preserved in Affaires Etrangères, Paris (Angleterre 81, f. 29), a document which, on inspection by the present writer at the French Foreign Office, provided no evidence whatever that the idea of re-union with Rome emanated from Charles II.

The other documents have to be judged on internal evidence, as supplied by

birth certificates, the first dated 'Whitehall, September 27, 1665,' a date when the Court was away from London owing to the Great Plague. The second certificate, dated 7th February, 1667, assigned a pension to the young man, provided he remained in London and adhered to the liturgy of the Church of England. But it appears that James had been brought up as a Calvinist, and as he prosecuted his studies, something like a miracle happened, because ' moved by grace and celestial light '[3] he suddenly realised that in Roman Catholicism was the sole guarantee of salvation. His conduct then became somewhat inconsequential. He left England (at the sacrifice of his pension) and went to Hamburg, where Cristina, the famous convert and ex-Queen of Sweden, was causing embarrassment to the Free City by antics similar to those which she normally performed in Rome. Why the devout young 'Prince,' at the moment of his conversion, should have selected this picturesque lady for his confidences is not clear, but the obliging Cristina gave him a certificate attesting not only his royal birth, but also his conversion to the Roman Catholic faith. On hearing of this, Charles was (justifiably) annoyed, because the ' secret ' would no longer be kept. Armed with his three royal certificates, James went to Rome where he was received as Novice by the Society of Jesus on April 11, 1668. Then followed the correspondence between Charles and the General

---

Boero's printed translations. Of these the most important are the five letters of Charles, said to be autograph, written by Charles to the General of the Jesuits. The present writer doubts their authenticity for these reasons:

(a) James de la Cloche before his conversion appears indifferently as a Calvinist or an Anglican. The distinction between such heresies might well appear indifferent to a Jesuit writing in Rome, but it would not have appeared indifferent to anyone living in Restoration England. Already Queen Elizabeth had been excommunicated as a *Calvinist*.

(b) The ominous date of the first birth certificate is repeated in the first letter of Charles to Oliva.

(c) In this letter Charles makes the extraordinary statement that he is writing in French ' so that no Englishman will get his nose into it.' Charles would never have thought that French was a sufficient disguise for a secret, nor would he ever have written such an incriminating statement.

(d) The five letters show a power of sustained literary exposition such as is unknown in the authentic letters of Charles II.

(e) Charles's ' secret '—namely, his imminent but always-delayed admission to the Roman Catholic Church—was a skilfully-played bargaining counter, associated more closely with money than with piety.

(f) Lastly, Father Boero's conception of truth, as revealed in his published writings, is not that entertained by the majority of educated men.

[3] Boero, *op. cit.*, p. 30.

(Oliva) the purport of which appears to be that the king intended to reserve great and secret matters for his son, whom he regarded with special affection, greater even than that which he was showing for Monmouth. Among these secret matters was that of the choice of an agent for the king's admission to the Roman Catholic Church. What better choice could be made for this purpose than the pious young novice, the king's first child? He was not yet a priest, but that difficulty could be overcome; moreover, once he had received his father into the Church, James might remain in London in order to administer the sacraments and provide spiritual direction for his royal parent. If Charles's Queen remained childless, and if the delicate children of the Duke of York died, then the kingdoms would descend to James de la Cloche, and Parliament could not lawfully object (!). The upshot of the correspondence was that the Novice, disguised as a Calvinist, went to London in November, 1668, but he remained there for less than a fortnight, and was sent back to the Jesuits in Rome with another 'secret' mission, the details of which are not revealed. After his return to Rome no more is heard of the royal Novice. Charles's last contribution to the subject is an I.O.U. for £800 payable to the Jesuits for the maintenance of his son during the few months of his stay in Rome, an extremely generous assessment of paternal obligation, explicable only when it is recalled that it was on behalf of a ' Prince,' and, after all, it was only an I.O.U. Of all Father Boero's documents this one does seem authentic.

These things may seem far removed from 'scientific' history and from Lord Acton, who more than any other historian insisted on proper authentication and assessment of original material:

> ' Method, not genius or eloquence or erudition, makes the historian. He may be discovered most easily by his use of authorities. The first question is whether the author understands the comparative value of sources of information, and has the habit of giving precedence to the most trustworthy informant.'[1]

Among Acton's informants was Father Boero, who at some period prior to 1862 supplied him with either the originals or copies of the

[1] Acton in *History of Freedom and Other Essays*, p. 235.

secret documents already referred to. The recipient at once realised
their importance. He noticed the awkward place and date of the
first birth certificate, but even this did not shake his faith. Further
research deepened the mystery. With the help of Kent's gossipy
Newsletters in the Record Office, and sources such as the Memoirs
of De Retz and of Guy Joli, and Clarke's *Life of James II* (all of
them notoriously unreliable) Acton was able to take up the story
where Boero had left off. The royal Novice had faded out of history
in November, 1668, but within a few weeks there appeared in Naples
a rich young man, claiming to be an Englishman, who began his
sensational career by marrying the daughter of his inn-keeper. His
profligate expenditure caused such suspicion that he was arrested,
and he then announced that he was Prince James Stuart, a son of
Charles II, born in Jersey. His wealth and the letters addressed to
him appeared to support this claim. The Viceroy thereupon com-
municated with Charles, who declared that the Neapolitan prisoner
was an impostor. Two days before his death in August, 1669, the
profligate James made an extraordinary will in which, besides
leaving enormous legacies to the Church and relatives, he demanded
the Principality of Wales for his son, who was not yet born. Father
Boero must indeed have been shocked when he was apprised of this
sequel, and Acton showed great ingenuity in his explanation of the
mystery. Clearly the Neapolitan impostor had good sources of
information; his money must have been obtained by robbery and
his information by stealing the Novice's papers containing Charles's
'secrets.' A mystery within a mystery! The real, the pious James
must have been somewhere else. He may, according to Lord Acton,
have continued, possibly under another name, in the work of preserving his father for the Faith; 'James Stuart's ministrations to his
father must have been confined to the discussion of Catholic
doctrines.'[1] He may, Acton conjectured, have been privy to the
'secret' of the Treaty of Dover (when Charles fooled Louis XIV);
he may, it was also suggested, have stood by his father's side during
the Popish Plot (when Charles uttered not a word of protest against
the many judicial murders of Roman Catholics whom he knew to
be innocent), but he was certainly not at the royal deathbed when,
at long last, Charles found in Father Huddlestone a person to whom

[1] Acton, in *Historical Essays and Studies*, p. 109.

he could confide his 'secret,' so long and skilfully exploited. With Teutonic erudition and perseverance Lord Acton searched every underground passage of late-seventeenth-century England for traces of the devout James, writing history not 'as it had actually happened,' but as it might conceivably have happened if we make the large assumption that both Father Boero's papers and Charles II's piety were genuine. A grain of humour would have saved the historian from this ponderous effort. The result was a series of stories as strange as any to which the sardonic Charles had been obliged in his lifetime to listen, episodes so confused and extraordinary that even their narrator confessed 'nobody knew what to believe.' These researches, embellished with a few curious anecdotes collected in his subterranean burrowings, and rounded off with a short discourse on toleration, in which he made the amazing statement that 'the Catholics [of the seventeenth century] had degenerated from the old mediæval spirit which stood by the right and respected the law, but did not stoop to power,'[1] were first published in *The Home and Foreign Review* (1862) under the title 'Secret History of Charles II.' In 1907 this nonsense was solemnly reprinted by Acton's editors in the collected *Historical Essays and Studies*.

It will be felt that this is merely a single example of how the piety of a great historian might outrun his judgment. But it is no solitary instance. Acton, the most erudite man of his generation, was also the most credulous. He surprised friends like John Morley by expressing belief in every story that came from Ireland, and by asking when Gladstone intended to place him (Acton) in the Cabinet.[2] Always preferring a devious to an obvious explanation, he suggested in his Memorandum for contributors to the *Cambridge Modern History* that those entrusted with the later periods might find 'secrets' in sources other than printed documents:

'Certain privately-printed memoirs may not be absolutely inaccessible, and there are elderly men about town gorged with esoteric information.'

Conscientious contributors, stimulated by the scientific standards formulated in the earlier part of the Memorandum, must have felt

---

[1] *Ibid.*, p. 121.   [2] Morley, in a conversation with Fisher, January 1, 1901.

troubled about such strange sources of 'esoteric' information; history-writing, at first promoted to the laboratory, was suddenly degraded to the gossip of the club-room and the backstairs. Nor was this all. Acton, one of the greatest moralists of his age, occasionally indulged in bouts of casuistry[1] which would have brought a blush of shame to the cheeks of his friend and admirer Mr. Gladstone, who always preserved a statesmanlike moderation in such matters. Most disquieting of all for any assessment of Acton's judgment is the reference in his inaugural lecture to the two men whom he proclaimed the greatest of living writers. One of these was Mommsen. *The other was Treitschke.*

Where he achieves his object, the 'scientific' or 'objective' historian does so not by piercing more deeply into the past, but by strictly limiting the scope of his enquiry. Selecting those aspects of history for which it is usually possible to find authenticated documents—for example, diplomatic history or administrative history—he undoubtedly achieves some degree of impartiality or neutrality, his critics would say colourlessness, the one respect in which Ranke can most easily be emulated. In effect, the principle of the 'scientific' historian is this: limit yourself to contemporary sources of undoubted authenticity; correlate them in order to eliminate error or discrepancy, and your unbiased exposition of the residium will be historic truth. But the kind of contemporary source here in question, whether the treaty or the statute or the proclamation, is often just the type of document which calls for explanation from other and less formal sources; for the terms of the treaty may

---

[1] Examples will be found in his review of Goldwin Smith's Irish History, reprinted in *History of Freedom and Other Essays*. These relate to the differences between the Protestant and the Catholic theories of persecution and to the circumstances in which the Pope can intervene between Prince and Subject, e.g.: 'Persecution is contrary to the nature of a universal church, it is peculiar to the national churches' (p. 254). 'There is no analogy between the persecution which preserves [presumably Roman Catholic persecution] and the persecution which attacks [presumably Protestant persecution], of intolerance as a religious duty and intolerance as a necessity of state' (p. 255). 'The idea of the Pope stepping between a state and the allegiance of its subjects is a mere misapprehension. The Pope could intervene only between the state and the occupant of the throne; and his intervention suspended, not the duty of obeying, but the right of governing. The line on which his sentence ran separated, not the subjects from the state, but the sovereign from the other authorities' (p. 257). The science of casuistry, even in its palmiest days of the seventeenth century, seldom went so far as this.

have little meaning without reference to the negotiations which preceded it or to the difficulties following its application; or the text may well be in foreign language, in the interpretation of which even the signatories themselves may attach different meanings to important phrases; so too, the statute may be so technical that the historian must abide by the interpretation of the lawyer, and he takes a risk if he tries to give its purport in language understandable by the layman, and as for the proclamation, it may merely illustrate another human characteristic—that of persisting in disobedience to a requirement of common or statute law. Or, look at it from the point of view of the future, when an enormous mass of literary material, now being accumulated by government departments, will be available for the historian. This material will be official and authentic, but much of it will also be non-committal, or may even have that anodyne quality found in the 'formula' which so often terminates one set of difficulties and starts another; all of it will necessarily preserve some detachment from the teeming and throbbing life which, after all, is the concern of the historian, who will be obliged to study that life at closer quarters than from the eminences of Whitehall or Westminster. It is when he leaves the official document that he will have to use sources of information on which he must exercise his judgment. Free and intelligent use of such less formal material is likely to make his interpretation of the past more valuable, but just because it is an interpretation, the less likely is it to be 'accurate' as that word is commonly used. Indeed, the most 'accurate' historical manuals are school text-books, provided the author avoids all but school text-books on the same subjects, and 'averages' every difference of opinion in his meagre sources. Still nearer to absolute accuracy is the list of dates.

As for the narration of events, of 'what actually happened,' that is the most treacherous of all. A trial in a modern law court will show how often a jury may have difficulty in deciding between the conflicting evidence of intelligent witnesses of an event, evidence which has been sifted out and analysed by counsel on both sides, or ruled out by the judge, and eventually the finding of the court may be reversed on appeal. The historian, where he does have the good fortune to discover contemporary accounts of the same event, cannot cross-question his witnesses; he cannot be sure of what they may have meant by a particular, and possibly vital, expression; he must act as philologist, counsel, jury and judge all rolled into one. It will be unfortunate if he thinks his finding definitive, and still more so if his readers make that assumption. The simple 'fact' is the most difficult of all things in history, for its expression is dependent on at least two sets of language—that of contemporary witnesses and that of the narrator, and language can never be a precision instrument.

Those who advocate the writing of 'absolute' history also assume that there is agreement about what constitutes history. On the contrary, this is subject to change and even fashion, for what interests us may not necessarily have interested our predecessors, and each age has its own view of what is historically important. As our interests are mainly economic, we are tempted to read economic motives into a past which professed, at least, to be guided by motives of a very different character. Or, to look again at the matter from the point of view which might be adopted in the future. There are things in our civilisation now for the first time recognised as important, about which we have evidence; will not the historian include these in 'history' in spite of the fact that they were ignored in the past? Of this an extreme instance may be quoted—the domestic fly, the subject of occasional reference by Homer and Old Testament writers, but unanimously considered unworthy of the notice of Clio. The fly may well have influenced the fate of campaigns in the past, but as we have no evidence, we omit. But now we know much more about the fly as a disease carrier, and no military historian can neglect the importance of such a scourge as dysentery in a desert campaign, a disease usually due to fly-infection. We can be sure, for instance, that the future historian of the war of 1939–45 will emphasise the vital importance of the battle of El Alamein—a turning-point in the war—and he is likely to do full justice to the strategy of the generals and the bravery of the men; but he may also, in the interests of truth, record how this great battle was preceded on the British side by a campaign against the fly, conducted by five officers and over two hundred men, with the result that 'there was a marked lowering of our dysentery-diarrhoea rate as compared with that of the enemy. At one time 40–50 per cent. of the enemy front-line troops were severely affected by dysentery or diarrhoea.'[1] And if a case can be substantiated for the inclusion in history writing of evidence about the fly, who can place the limits of enquiry beyond which the historian must not go? Will not this increasing necessity for selection emphasise still more the imponderable, human factor in the historian? History is 'true' only in so far as it is the reflection of the past in the mirror of the writer's personality; Fisher's *History of Europe* reflects a personality which was intelligent, well-informed and sane.

The question of Fisher's reliability is still unanswered. Some of the criticisms which reached him privately serve to suggest how historic 'truth' is often no more than a matter of opinion, varying with race and religion, and sometimes subordinated to considerations of policy. Of the last point an example is provided in Fisher's treatment of the Reformation in England (Book II, ch. IX). Rightly or wrongly, he deliberately avoided committing himself to anything controversial, and as he had no case to make for any church or creed he at least tried to avoid giving offence. In the lists of books which he appended to this chapter he included works by Cardinal Gasquet and Hilaire Belloc as well as books by Protestant writers, which at least suggests that he was trying to be impartial. But a Protestant clergyman, writing to Fisher, contended that in the interests of 'truth' the author should have given a ruling on the Gasquet-Coulton controversy, to which Fisher does not even refer. As a matter of fact, Fisher had made up his mind on the rights and wrongs of that controversy, but he was much too politic to intervene, so the 'truth' must be sought elsewhere. His evasion was not always so fortunate. The account of Mahomet and Mahommedanism (Book I, ch. XII) appears to most Europeans acceptable, and even conventional. But a distinguished Mahommedan scholar wrote to him in these terms:

'The chapter on Islam is the least satisfactory of all, and the character sketch of the prophet Mohammed is so misleading and prejudiced that no Muslim can read it without pain and distress. The chapter on India is equally unsatisfactory. It is not history but propaganda.'

[1] H. S. Gear 'Hygiene Aspects of the El Alamein Victory' in *British Medical Journal*, March 18, 1944.

As Fisher offended Muslims, so he offended Jews. In his account of conditions in Germany immediately after 1918 he referred to the old soldiers who were ' miserably needy and often despised by Jewish profiteers.'[1] This was stigmatised by a Professor of the Hebrew University of Jerusalem as ' a gross insult to the 12,000 German-Jewish soldiers killed in the War.' Similar objection was made by another critic to Fisher's suggestion[2] that the British policy of creating a home for the Jews in Palestine rallied to the Allied cause the financial help of ' the powerful and cosmopolitan community which controls the loan markets of the world.' To the complainant this seemed to conceal and even distort the idealist element underlying British policy and the Balfour Declaration. Fisher, one of the most enlightened and liberal-minded of men, had offended both Jews and Mohammedans by ' untrue ' and even insulting statements about them; he may unwittingly have given similar offence to Hindus and Confucians, whose silence must not be interpreted as evidence of approval. Of this we can be certain, that Fisher, politic as he was, did not possess that gift, exemplified so brilliantly by some historians, of writing in such a way as to give complete satisfaction to everyone.

These criticisms give point to a question which has notoriously baffled mankind since before the days of Pontius Pilate—what is truth? While the physicist has long been accustomed to think of space as multidimensional, and of direction and velocity as relative to the observer, many critics, thinking in linear terms, consider history to be the exact dilineation in language of a continuous progression or sequence, ignoring the obvious conclusion that as the past included an infinitely great number of observers or agents, there must have been an equally great number of reactions to the impact of what, for want of a better word, we call ' events.' Truth is not always simple, or absolute or universal. A cynic described it as ' le mensonge qui dure '; it was defined by a saint (Joan of Arc) as ' something for telling which men are often hanged '; indeed, the prickly plant of truth, which yields its rare blossoms only to the poets, readily sheds its spines on admitted failures and prospective martyrs. Of the latter Lord Curzon very nearly provided an example. When about to publish his great book *Persia and the*

---

[1] *History of Europe*, p. 1205.   [2] *Ibid.*, p. 114.

Persian Question, he was appointed Under Secretary of State for India (1891), and in view of derogatory remarks in his manuscript about the Shah the question of their publication by a member of the Government was raised. To Curzon's protest that the remarks were true Lord Salisbury, endowed with the accumulated wisdom of centuries, replied that this was precisely the circumstance which made their publication intolerable.[1] Later in life Curzon made the discovery that, just as morality may vary with the latitude, so truth may change with the longitude, a superior variety in the west, an inferior variety in the east, a discovery which he announced with startling results to the assembled convocation of the University of Calcutta.[2] Too often the truth is not what the writer thinks, but what the public wants, and so scholarship may yield place to show-manship.

Looked at from this broad point of view, there are general pronouncements in the *History of Europe* the truth of which is at least debatable. When we apply the opposite method and examine statements, as it were, microscopically, the results are even more disquieting. A correspondent complained that Fisher's references to Mr. Gladstone contained nearly as many mistakes as words. Now if there was anyone about whom Fisher ought to have been right it was Mr. Gladstone, so this accusation must be examined, if only to show the snares that may underlie the simplest and least rhetorical statements of 'fact'. On p. 1043 Gladstone is referred to as 'a large landlord,' and on p. 1044 there is an antithesis between Disraeli 'a Hebrew adventurer of genius' and Gladstone 'a High Church English squire.' Close examination shows that these apparently innocent descriptions bristle with difficulties, and possibly errors. First of all, Gladstone the large landlord. Contemporaries were familiar with pictures and even bas-reliefs depicting the Grand Old Man vigorously felling trees, and they naturally assumed that the trees were his own, growing on his own land. But that this was merely circumstantial evidence is shown by reference to Morley's *Life*[3] from which it appears that the great statesman, in order to help his brother-in-law, Sir Stephen Glynne, who was financially embarrassed, devoted the bulk of his fortune to the task of keeping

[1] Earl of Ronaldshay (Lord Zetland), *Life of Lord Curzon*, I, pp. 154-5.
[2] *Ibid.*, II, p. 363. [3] Book III, ch. 2.

Hawarden in the family, and with this object he was for a short time the unwilling owner of the Hawarden estates. But he had scruples against landowning, possibly on the ground that it might interfere with his public duties, and when he did unexpectedly succeed to the reversion of Hawarden he speedily transferred it to his eldest son. These complicated transactions caused him such effort and anxiety that, in his own words, 'they would run to a volume.' Fortunately he did not write the volume, but the fact remains that Gladstone was a large landowner for only a few years, and that with extreme, even gladstonian, compunction. Hence also it is doubtful whether he could properly be described as a 'squire.'

'English squire' according to Fisher's critic is even more questionable, for Gladstone was of Scottish ancestry (with a Scandinavian element if one goes back far enough), and moreover Hawarden is in Wales, not England. But most difficult of all is the epithet 'High Church.' What were Mr. Gladstone's religious principles? Now, on this subject he had written a book,[1] but it had made confusion worse confounded, and had prompted Daniel O'Connell to declare that its author was progressing—towards Rome. The Evangelicals appear to have disliked Gladstone because of his dogmatic rigour; the old-fashioned Protestants distrusted him because of his dallyings with the Vatican, and some Anglo-Catholics regarded him as at best a bad friend; indeed, one is tempted to resolve the problem of his real convictions by claiming that he was the Jekyll and Hyde of Victorian politics, his virtues exemplified in Protection, Churchmanship and Unionism, his backslidings in Free Trade, Disestablishment and Home Rule. But even such a refinement over-simplifies matters, for this Dr. Jekyll, when accused of leading a double life, would reply in long speeches, the body of which was a scathing denunciation of sin, while the parentheses amounted to a complete exculpation of his partner Mr. Hyde. It cannot be pretended that Fisher has done anything like justice to such a richly diversified personality, but at least on this count of the indictment—that he was wrong in calling Gladstone a High Churchman—one can return a Scottish verdict of Not Proven. If such a microscopic method of examination be applied to every statement in Fisher's 1200 pages, one may be tempted to conclude that

[1] *Church and State* (1839).

the only reliable part of the book is the index, and that was not his work.

Of the more general objections which have been urged against Fisher's book one is that a history of Europe compressible into a single volume stands self-condemned. Something must obviously have been left out, so its size alone may appear evidence that it is no more than a manual for the delectation of the uncritical rather than for the enlightenment of the scholar. That Fisher should have taken the very serious (academic) risk of writing such a book is one of the many illustrations of the French element in his temperament, for in France the word *vulgarisation* does not have the opprobrious implication of the English equivalent, and French historians of highest repute have not thought it beneath their dignity to write general surveys which might be described as 'popular.' Still more, it has usually been recognised in France that the writing of text-books, so far from being the preserve of the hack writer, should almost as a matter of duty be done by the best-accredited historians. The result is that in several subjects, including history, French text-books are remarkable for lucidity, skilful arrangement of subject-matter, and avoidance of the prolix and the irrelevant, qualities in which Fisher excelled; and indeed this may be the main reason why the *History of Europe* has not yet been translated into French, since Frenchmen have for so long been familiar with books which unite scholarship with clarity, readableness and brevity, whereas we have always been encouraged to dissociate these qualities. Many of us are distrustful of anything which tends to make the path of learning, particularly historical learning, so interesting that we are tempted to follow it to the end, and as men are sometimes penalised as much for their virtues as for their vices, so Fisher's good qualities as a historian often provide the real reason why his compendium is unacceptable to those who cannot bring themselves to believe that history should be both intelligent and intelligible.

Other serious objections have been raised to a book which has never been popular in the academic world. One is that Fisher presents no theory of history; he finds no clue to unravel the complicated skein of human achievement and folly; indeed, he disclaims any knowledge of such a clue. He might have stimulated the interest of the reader by suggesting analogies between numerous scattered events never before inter-connected, a specialised occupation making heavier demands on learning and ingenuity than on other and humbler qualities; or he might have given a unity to the book by referring the sequence of events to some single, underlying cause, preferably economic in character. Many of us have been taught at school to think of history as so unintelligent and distasteful that we eagerly welcome the book which tells us why things happened, and he is indeed fortunate who can explain the causes of things. Most of the literature professing to find an economic explanation of history is based on the doctrines of Karl Marx, and many writers, from this starting-point, think of human evolution only in terms of class conflict. It is because such history-writing is preferred by a large body of serious-minded readers to the kind of history which Fisher wrote, that a reference to it must here be made, with this clear distinction that the literature here in question is quite different from the writing of straightforward economic history, in which so much of permanent value has been achieved. Fisher, it should be noted, attached great importance to social and economic factors, but he held that these were by no means the only things accountable for the conduct of men or the sequence of events.

A glance at Fisher's account of the Great Rebellion in seventeenth-century England (Book II, ch. 19) will show that he attributed this movement mainly to religious and constitutional causes, and so too with the sixteenth-century Reformation, which he connected with things of the mind and spirit. To many such an interpretation will appear grievously out of date. He seems almost to ignore class interest and economic motive. An investigation of those writers who have applied either 'sociological' or Marxian conceptions to the interpretation of history will show that three main classes are in evidence—a 'proletariat' of workers, dependent on wages; a capitalist middle class or bourgeoisie, exploiting the workers, and distinguished by a narrow, canting morality; and thirdly, an aristocracy, cultured and effete, subsisting without effort on the produce of the two lower classes. Such a simple, static type of society may have existed in certain parts of Europe in the days of Karl Marx, and if we begin by assuming (as many writers do) that it has always existed in the past, then a great deal will follow *logically*. Starting with such a rigid classification we shall interpret history in terms of class conflict, and in this way the past becomes not only more interesting to the intelligent reader, but it possesses more 'actuality,' since we obtain historical confirmation of our own social or economic views. If the reasoning of such books is not always very clear, that is not necessarily an objection, because our own failure to understand a book may seem proof of our own intellectual inferiority to the author, and accordingly we may be tempted to hold him in higher esteem.

Among the most notable of those who have related history to class and race is Professor Werner Sombart, well known to English readers from translations of his books. A glance at one of the best known, that on Capitalism,[1] will show how many things hitherto obscure can be simply explained. Thus we are assured that the citizens of Florence became the foremost of traders in the Middle Ages, not from any fortuitous advantage of situation or aptitude, but 'because of their Etruscan and Greek (i.e. Oriental) blood.'[2] The student of Italian history may well ask why Florence should be selected as an illustration of the connection between Greek or Oriental blood and pre-eminence in trade, since Florence was noted as much for its industries and for the backing of its highly developed agricultural neighbourhood, whereas the Levantine and trading elements are more clearly exemplified in Genoa and Venice. As for the Etruscan element, all that is known for certain is that ancient Etruscan civilisation was more highly developed than contemporary civilisations in Italy. Dr. Sombart, however, gives us an example from nearer home:

> 'As for the Scotch, if there is any truth that the Frisians settled on the eastern shores of Scotland, are we not justified in asserting that the Scots have preserved their peculiar national traits from the very earliest period in their history? The Frisians, so much is certain, were a clever and skilful race of traders.'[3]

But Dr. Sombart himself admits a difficulty in this simple explanation of 'the peculiar national traits' of the Scots, for there is a strong Celtic element in Scotland, and both sociologists and economists are

[1] W. Sombart, *The Quintessence of Capitalism*, translated by M. Epstein (1915).
[2] *Ibid.*, p. 215.   [3] *Ibid.*, p. 216.

agreed that the Scottish Celt is not suited for commerce (in contrast with the French Celt), and indeed the Celts of the North, it has to be admitted, preferred to earn their living by the more aristocratic occupation of cattle raiding. But this difficulty is overcome by the fact that, apparently in the fifteenth century, most of the Celtic nobility of Southern Scotland conveniently removed themselves to the more congenial atmosphere of the Highlands—'those of the nobility that could saved themselves by removing to the Highlands. The result was that the Frisian trading element became predominant in the Lowlands.'[1] This important migration appears to have escaped the notice of the historians of Scotland. In another book, *Der Bourgeois*, Professor Sombart claims that the Scots were 'the Florentiners of the North,' a phrase which Scottish readers will find more acceptable than the following curious analogy:

> 'Just as in history the elevation of the Medici is the only instance of bankers becoming territorial princes, so it has happened only once in history that a nation has sold its king to a foreign country, as the Scots sold Charles I.'[2]

When a nation sells even its kings to foreigners, what better proof could be had of commercial aptitude?

Professor Sombart's books have been selected for quotation because they have such a wide publicity in this country. More formidable are the Marxians. They would quickly dispose of Dr. Sombart's attribution of Scottish commercial genius to the 'Frisian' element by showing that Calvinism was the real cause, since, under the cloak of religion, the Scottish preachers (we are told) constantly enjoined on their bourgeois flocks the moral duty of making money and lending it out at usurious rates of interest. As for the 'eternally damned,' in predestinarian Scotland that theological expression was merely a polite name used by the bourgeoisie for their 'wage slaves.' All are agreed that, historically, Scotland like Holland was economically prosperous; there is difference only about the cause. But the humble student of Scottish history has to confess that, until late in the eighteenth century, Scotland was one of the poorest and most undeveloped countries in Europe.

[1] *Ibid.*, p. 218.   [2] *Der Bourgeois* (1923), p. 129.

Marxian assumptions have been applied with even greater ingenuity to the study of seventeenth-century England, notably by Dr. Max Weber,[1] whose disciples have converted the majority of English students to the view that the religious and political phraseology of both Puritan and Royalists were merely a blind for motives of economic or class interest. Dr. Weber has claimed that Stuart Anglicanism, especially as practised by Laud, was characterised by 'social organisation in the fiscal-monopolistic form,' while the Puritans, such as Prynne, 'repudiated all connection with the large-scale capitalistic courtiers as an ethically suspicious class.'[2] The quotation does not read more easily in the original German, and needs thinking out. Prynne and his fellow Puritans, the author continues, 'took pride in their own superior middle-class business morality, which formed the true reason for the persecutions to which they were subjected.' In other words, Prynne was persecuted not as he himself supposed for his *Histriomastix* or for his violent speeches in the Commons but because Laud and his monopolistic colleagues of the Star Chamber objected to his 'middle-class business morality.' Hard things have been said of Laud, but never anything so hard as this, and incidentally, students of the period may recall how Laud in the Star Chamber often protected the smallholder against the enclosures of the large landlord. But the choice of Prynne as a Puritan 'business man,' acting in what he considered the interests of himself or his class, is not only a singularly unfortunate one for the Marxian thesis, but a specially relevant one for the other thesis, that history is more usually made by men who ignore their economic or class interest; for no one had less to do with business than 'scripturiant' Prynne, nor did anyone ever illustrate more vividly how some men, and important men too, may spend active lives consistently engaged in headlong defiance of their own obvious interests, whether economic or not. Trained originally as a barrister, Prynne divided his time between the House of Commons and prison, with brief, turbulent intervals on a small farm near Bath, writing books and pamphlets all the time, none of them showing any interest in trade or business, their author invariably engaged on a course of conduct certain to involve him in pecuniary loss, professional discredit,

[1] *The Protestant Ethic and the Spirit of Capitalism*, English translation (1930).
[2] *Ibid.*, p. 179.

facial mutilation and acute personal discomfort, until at the Restoration he was appointed Keeper of the Records in the Tower, where he gave nine years of devoted service for two years' salary. So far from exemplifying a narrow 'bourgeois morality' Prynne was one of the finest exponents of unselfish devotion to what he considered great causes. Nor is he a solitary example of this, and only by excluding all such men from our survey can we reduce human motive, as revealed in history, to the sordid level of economic self-interest. But nevertheless the fact has to be recognised that Dr. Weber's interpretation of the period—more reasonably and moderately expressed than that of most Marxians—is the one which now holds the field.

Academic disciples of the Marxians are numerous. Some express themselves with such vagueness and caution that their statements often amount to little more than this, that if the causes of great historical events are seriously and scientifically examined they will be found economic. There is at least safety in this method of writing history. Others, more enterprising, make free use of mathematical or scientific analogies intended to prove that economic factors provide the sole or ultimate explanation of historical evolution, forgetting that a scientific analogy, particularly where it betrays deficient knowledge of elementary science, is not a proof.[1] There is undoubtedly a sense in which it is true to say that the basis of human life is economic, the same rudimentary sense in which it can be described as physiological, and at times life may be reduced to the minimum functions of eating and breathing, both of which, while they are obviously necessities of civilisation, are not necessarily adequate explanations of all the phenomena of civilisation. Of those who offer more concrete information one writer,[2] following Dr. Weber, has recently suggested that the disputes over monopolies illustrate the real character of the English Revolution, since in these disputes we have the antagonism of two types of economic organisa-

[1] For examples see G. Plekhanov, *Fundamental Problems of Marxism* (1928), particularly p. 97, where the author, in support of his view that sudden changes and revolutions are natural, makes the unfortunate selection of water reduced to ice by cold and water raised to vapour by heat as examples of 'sudden' changes in Nature. The examples cited merely prove that Nature is a bad Marxian, for she resists change of state.

[2] C. Hill, in *The English Revolution* (1940), pp. 36–40.

tion—the large-scale, exclusive enterprise, often in the hands of a courtier, and the small, struggling businesses of the Puritan ' bourgeoisie,' threatened with extinction by the more privileged and powerful organisation. From this point of view, phrases like ' religious freedom' and ' constitutional liberty' are ruled out altogether, and the great seventeenth-century conflict is reduced to economic terms :

> ' There was a great deal of capital in England which merchants and gentlemen were anxious to invest in the freest possible industrial, commercial and agricultural development. This was continually thwarted by feudal survivals in town and country, and by government policy deliberately endeavouring, in the interests of the old landed, ruling class, to restrict production and the accumulation of capital. Thus, in attacking the feudal order and the oligarchy of big merchants in alliance with the Court who were trying to monopolise business profits, the struggle of the bourgeoisie was progressive. . . . The interests of the new class of capitalist merchants and farmers were temporarily identical with those of the small peasantry and artisans and journeymen. . . . The monarchy was bound up with the feudal order by more than the bonds of conservative sentiment. The king was himself the greatest of feudal landlords and, though he was in a better position than any other feudalist to get a rake-off from the new capitalist wealth, he was opposed no less than any other landowner to a fundamental change from a feudal to a capitalist order of society.'

The above sentences have been selected as a fair example of the kind of thesis which is most popular to-day. It is perhaps immaterial that it is not supported by the citation of any historical evidence from the seventeenth century; indeed, it is a tacit assumption of the Marxians that such notable evidence as the Petition of Right, the Agreement of the People and the Bill of Rights (in all of which economic grievance is overshadowed by religious, political and legal principle) cannot be considered a true expression of the real motives of the actors in the constitutional struggle. Briefly, the purport of the above quotation appears to be that there was much capital in early-Stuart England; that merchants and others wanted opportunities for free investments and development; that in this they were constantly thwarted by the Crown in alliance with large monopolists and effete survivors of the 'feudal system;' that the progressive elements were in temporary alliance with the small peasantry and journeymen; and that the king, though not unwilling to have a 'rake-off' from his 'feudal' opportunities, was opposed to a change from a 'feudal' to a 'capitalistic' order of society. Hence the English Revolution.

Expressed in these clear terms, the artificiality of the economic interpretation becomes obvious. Certain characteristically modern conceptions are shifted bodily into the earlier seventeenth century, where they are naturally found to be in conflict with the remnants of another system—the 'feudal system.' The fact is ignored that in a community where capitalism, as we know it, was still in its infancy, the desire for free investment must have been much less than it is to-day. In agriculture the fallacy is even more patent, for 'improving' on anything like a large scale did not begin until after 1760, and moreover, the reference to 'the old landed ruling class' will appear strange to those who bear in mind the extent of the recent Tudor confiscations, and the rise of a new territorial nobility. Nor is it by any means clear why the peasantry and journeymen should have thrown in their lot, even temporarily, with the 'progressive' bourgeoisie, especially as, according to the economic thesis, every man acts in the interests of himself or his class. But most difficult of all is the application of the thesis to the Crown. So far from the king having a 'rake-off' from his feudal opportunities, the situation, as historians have long known, was exactly the reverse, for the Crown lands were utterly insufficient to pay for the greatly increased cost of government. As for the king setting himself against the new capitalist order, and sacrificing himself on behalf of those who opposed that order, we shall be obliged, if the thesis is true, to admit that Charles I died not on behalf of the Church of England, but in defiance of the Stock Exchange.

Disputes over monopolies were undoubtedly important in the reigns of Elizabeth and the early Stuarts,[1] but they played only a small part in a revolution which, extending over a generation, assumed completely different forms, none of them due solely or even

[1] They lost many of their irritant characteristics in 1624 when a statute transferred jurisdiction over them to the Common Law.

mainly to economic causes. There was, for example, the learned, almost pedantic opposition to the Stuarts maintained by such men as Coke, Selden and Eliot, an opposition based on appeal to common-law precedents; there was the bitter hostility of the Puritans to the ritualist Laud and the Star Chamber; after 1643 there was the opposition of the Independents, uneducated and thoroughgoing, imbued most of all by hatred by the professions, including those of king, bishop, priest, lord of parliament and, most of all, lawyer; then followed the Second Civil War in which men like Prynne (a Presbyterian, not a Puritan) were ranged with the Scots on the side of the Monarchy and the Lords against an Army composed mainly of Independents; and finally there was the Commonwealth and the rule of Cromwell, a leader who, surrounded by men constantly receiving revelations from on high, saw to it that the revelation accorded to him was the one acted upon. To allege that all these things were merely subtle disguises for the cloaking of economic motive, whether of an individual or of a class, is to do a gross injustice not only to English history but to English character. Fisher's presentation of history may often seem old-fashioned, or devoid of those 'clever' explanations which find such a ready welcome to-day, but it is richer in human interest than any 'interpretation' offered by either the German Marxians or their English disciples, and to that extent it is more true.

From another point of view it can be argued that Fisher's *History of Europe* is not up to date. He had ended his study of the subject in 1912, and thereafter his many duties had prevented him from keeping pace with the great flow of historical literature, and so in the twenty years preceding the writing of the book he had been able to read only in his spare time. Inevitably, books of importance, chiefly monographs, were unread, a number were even unknown to him, with the result that he had to base his survey mainly on what he had read before 1912. In many academic circles this is regarded as fatal, and the *History of Europe* has in some quarters been dismissed as unreliable, because it is based almost entirely on 'old' books.

But it is not certain that this disability is so serious as is usually maintained. Insistence on the very latest books is understandable in the scientific subjects, where so much depends on research, but in a subject like history, where newly-available original material of importance bears a very small proportion to that already in use, research is not always bound to upset older verdicts, and fresh interpretations of existing material may sometimes leave the reader more convinced of his original opinion. Of this one clear example may be cited. William the Silent has recently been the subject of much new investigation based on contemporary sources, and two opposite verdicts have been given by Protestant writers of well-established repute. As they were published after the publication of the *History*, they should now, on the argument commonly adduced, have an even greater importance than those enunciated in the twenty years before Fisher wrote. One of the verdicts[1] is this:

' He is one of that small band of statesmen whose service to humanity is greater than their service to their time or their people.'

Here is the other:[2]

' This coarse and brutal materialist has often been transformed by religious and political partisanship into an angel of light on the ground that he stood almost alone on the side of religious toleration in an age that refused it. In reality his tolerance was due not to any moral or intellectual superiority to his age, but to his need of certain allies within and without the Netherlands who held widely divergent religious views. To see him as a paladin of political or religious equality for the proletariat is grotesquely to misunderstand both William and his age.'

Now both these opinions are based on the study of original sources, and the explanation of religious bias has to be excluded. Had Fisher read them, he would probably have decided to leave untouched his own verdict,[3] which recognises the difficulty of coming to a conclusion about so complex a character.

William the Silent recalls another subject about which much has recently been written—sixteenth-century Spain. If Fisher had read

[1] C. V. Wedgwood, *William the Silent* (1944), p. 253.
[2] Rev. R. Trevor Davies, *The Golden Age of Spain* (1937), p. 156.
[3] *History of Europe*, p. 589.

such a good monograph as J. Klein's *The Mesta* he would have learned much about Spanish social and economic life in the later middle ages, but how far he could have utilised this valuable information in the space at his disposal is another matter. Had he been encouraged to proceed further with some of the newer books, he might have been surprised and even distressed to learn that the Moriscos, hitherto regarded as an intelligent and hard-working community, were really on no higher plane than Hottentots, or to use the comparison actually suggested, American Negroes, and that, as they resented the proceedings taken for their conversion and were suspected of adopting measures to defend themselves, they deserved the harsh persecution and expulsion to which they were subjected by pious rulers. From another recent book he would have received the assurance that much of the greatness of Spain, intellectual as well as material, was due to the Spanish Inquisition; elsewhere, he would have been told that our modern jury system owes a great deal to the judicial procedure and sense of fairness which, it is claimed, were characteristic of that tribunal. Had he succeeded in absorbing these new points of view, advocated by recent English and American writers, he would have had less difficulty in swallowing the suggestion that our modern doctrine of 'the will of the people' can be fathered on those Spanish Jesuits who advocated tyrannicide. Nor would such surprises have been limited to the history of Spain, since Fisher would have found a similar novelty in some recent interpretations of our own history, particularly Stuart history, for example, the discovery that Charles II was distinguished by two typically British virtues—patriotism and economy in money matters, and that Jeffreys was really an upright judge, handicapped by a keen sense of humour. Indeed, had he been able to keep pace with historical output, Fisher might have noted an increasing number of books, written seriously for serious students, devoted not only to the condonation but to the applauding of what he knew by instinct to be brutality and bigotry. The *History of Europe* was written only just in time, for it is a last, graceful expression of a civilisation now rapidly passing away.

For the purpose to which Fisher set himself, the practical experience of men of affairs which he obtained in the years after 1912 was a far better supplement to his literary equipment than the

attempt to keep in touch with all the newer books. And his equipment was elaborate. It included an intimate acquaintance with the
historical and general literature of ancient Greece and Rome; of
England, France, Germany and Italy, both mediæval and modern;
it was amplified by profound knowledge of the Mediæval Empire
and Napoleonic Europe, a knowledge so skilfully used that one can
never tell where the general historian ends and the specialist begins;
it was an equipment not merely of knowledge, but of well-chosen
knowledge, extending over centuries and continents, and disposed
by an intellect never profound, but always balanced, shrewd and
wise. Hence at this point it is reasonable to alter the question about
Fisher's accuracy into one more relevant to the task which he undertook—namely, was his judgment sound? The book stands or falls
by the answer to this question.

One is encouraged to give a favourable answer by the knowledge
that Fisher possessed the judicial quality in a remarkable degree,
due not to formal training, but to his temperament, which was
detached, dispassionate, impersonal and sometimes almost institu-
tional. Nor was it merely that he took into account what could be
said on both sides of a question, for most of us habitually do that;
what distinguished Fisher was that he knew the essential things to
be taken into account when determining questions arising from
twenty-five centuries of European history, and his choice of the
facts requisite for his purpose was invariably dictated by common-
sense. It is this quality, rather than any completeness of formal
'correctness' of statement, which gives to the book its value and
truth. In consequence he was often right where the specialist was
wrong. An important instance may be cited. During the inter-war
years some scholars were inclined to accept the German view about
the 'war guilt' of 1914, or more often to compromise and declare
that all parties shared the guilt. A historian[1] possessing unrivalled
knowledge both of German history and of European displomacy has
written thus:

> 'The War was the child of European anarchy, of the outworn
> system of sovereign states. The Old World had degenerated into
> a powder magazine.... It is a mistake to attribute exceptional de-

---

[1] Dr. G. P. Gooch, *Recent Revelations in European Diplomacy* (4th edition,
1940), p. 470.

pravity to any of the governments which, in the words of Mr. Lloyd George, stumbled and staggered into the war.'

Now such an opinion at once commends itself to English readers by its very reasonableness and moderation, by its spirit of fairness to the ex-enemy, by the corroboration of a statesman most closely in touch with events, and by our knowledge that it is based on impartial investigation of original papers. But, unfortunately, we are not living in a reasonable or moderate age, and the above-quoted verdict is not only wrong, but very wrong, because it ignores three things of vital importance in any assessment of the *responsibility* of the governments concerned (not their *depravity* which no one has ever even alleged)—namely, the many and even desperate attempts made by this country to secure a basis for peace; secondly, the impossibility of finding out what Germany really wanted; and most important of all, the long intellectual and material preparation for war with which Germany began hostilities in 1914. Fisher never had any doubts on this question:

> 'The one power in Europe which could have ensured peace refused its co-operation in the endeavours which were made to obtain it. The German government, which might have prevented the war, took the responsibility of declaring it. . . . It was idle to suppose that they [the German people] would recall the many occasions in recent history when their own government had sought to obtain its diplomatic ends by threats of war or the apprehension which had been excited in foreign lands by its imperialism.'[1]

This view, not generally accepted by historians at the time of its enunciation, has been amply justified by more recent events.

The same events have confirmed the soundness of Fisher's judgment in another and much less obvious way. Platonist and agnostic, he found in the long record of European civilisation not the workings of Providence, nor the continuity of Progress, but a continual ebb and flow by which the summits of human achievement are alternately revealed or obscured. He believed that events are shaped not in accordance with any set of principles, but by

[1] *History of Europe*, p. 1118.

contact of circumstance with the dynamic, even daemonic force of human personality. Confronted with a problem which has baffled greater men, he took refuge in a paradox, the paradox of the irrationality of *homo sapiens*. This interpretation of history, such as it is, was given abundant illustration in his later years and still more in the years which succeeded his death in 1940, for in that period was witnessed the awesome spectacle of the rise and fall of a great state, richly endowed, highly civilised and laboriously educated, a state actuated not by those motives of economic interest or commercial rivalry which can be gauged by accepted standards, nor by grievances which may be remedied by concession or compromise, but dominated and energised by primitive forces of evil so closely and persistently identified with good, that at the command of a leader and his associates black became white, wrong became right, and all the accepted canons not merely of Christian civilisation but of human decency were whirled around in a wild phantasmagoria in which the *Zeitgeist* was a *Poltergeist* and the Devil was God. The language of theology is the least inadequate for description of these happenings of our own times. Half consciously Fisher had applied to the Europe which he knew an almost Manichean conception of the continual and intimate interplay of the twin forces of good and evil, an interplay usually having no greater inconvenience than that of making more difficult our valuation of human motive, but capable at times of producing revolution and disaster. For sacrifice can easily be transferred from divine to satanic altars, and the worshipper may himself be least aware of the transmutation in the object of his devotions, for that object is still a god, and therefore all who minister at its shrine must be good, and all who are indifferent or hostile are necessarily evil. Hence the ever-recurrent possibility of a subtle alliance between statecraft and religion—' if they were kings, they were also priests; if they were wicked, they were also holy.'

It is in this respect that Fisher recalls Gibbon. Both, while enjoying moderately good health, had that valetudinarian temperament which, by the imposition of strict regime, makes more easily possible the accumulation of vast stores of learning; both in the calm tenour of their lives were spared the fierce joys, and still more the devastating reactions, which may follow from passion and emotion.

Neither was a thinker but both, supreme as expositors, were the embodiments and exponents of great civilisations, the one a product of eighteenth-century scepticism, the other a posthumous child of Gladstonian Liberalism. Neither would have sacrificed himself for a losing cause, still less for a lost one, because their mission was not to reform the present nor to shape the future but, by interpreting the past, each in the flawless mirror of his own personality, to make more clear to their fellow-men the deeper implications of the age in which they lived. Aloof and detached, they unrolled vast panoramas of human history, with a crystal-like clarity such as men had not known since the days of Tacitus, the one fascinating or revolting by a Voltairean cynicism, the other, more restrained, alternately charming or perturbing by occasional peeps of a delicate irony wherewith he hinted at the perennial contrast between profession and practice. Such an attitude may appear least acceptable in an age frantically striving to replace the essentials of civilisation, and to preserve them from a menace greater even than any which Fisher knew. But he had much to say about these essentials and, if we have anything to learn from the past, we can learn something from the *History of Europe*; for, as in no other book, aggression is judged not by its immediate success, but by its remoter disasters; civilisation is assessed by its quality, not by its material force; the individual is regarded as always superior to the average of the mass; the well-being and progress of humanity are linked not with the heroic or aspiring virtues of unswerving conviction and invariable principle, but with the ordinary instincts of toleration, forbearance and good sense; and, lastly, on the common heritage of European culture, shared alike by France and Germany, by the British Commonwealth of Nations and the United States of America, is imposed a solemn trusteeship for the civilisation of the world. It is in this sense that Fisher's *History of Europe* is an intensely moral book.

X

Conclusion

Two distinguished scientists have agreed that ' so long as there is a normal man alive he will continue to be lord of the world.'[1] The normal man is he who, while distrusting the eccentrics of his own generation, and refraining from any course of conduct which might place him in an unpopular minority, nevertheless accepts and applies those ideas of deceased eccentrics and minorities which have become essential parts of our social inheritance. Normality, as thus considered, is not only the constituent which binds together our social fabric but, in the sense of complete or instinctive adaptation to environment, it is the quality, usually described as *savoir faire*, which ensures personal success in the conditions of civilised life, and promotes stability and continuity when that civilisation threatens to break down. It is the normal man who reaps what the pioneer and martyr have sown, a fact which may have been in the mind of Aristotle when in the *Politics* he declared that the good of things must be that which preserves them. From this point of view Fisher was one of the most normal men of all time.

In only two respects did he vary from normality. The first was his Agnosticism, which in a private memorandum he described as Atheism. Disbelief in any of the accepted creeds is no longer a serious bar in all the professions, but it is still to some extent a social disability, for in many influential quarters the religious sceptic is considered either perverse or depraved, from which imputations Fisher was saved by public knowledge of his balanced judgment and invariable integrity. But this fact, always kept in the background, did serve to distinguish him from the majority of those with whom he came into contact, and made it more difficult for others to understand him fully, because such a profound difference from his fellow-

[1] F. Wood Jones, F.R.S., and S. D. Porteus, *The Matrix of the Mind* (1929), p. 412.

men helped to deepen his reserve. Convinced that the various creeds merely created deities in the image of their worshippers, he was unable to join with those who publicly pay lip service to doctrines which either they do not believe or accept only in a very nominal sense. Himself a man of compromise, he considered this one immoral. An idealist, he conscientiously refused allegiance to doctrinal requirements which, in the view of so many thinking men, have accounted for all that is best in the past, and are thought to provide the only guarantee of whatever may prove to be good in the future. All this helped to make Fisher somewhat solitary—a Platonist who had wandered into a convocation of communicants, many of them with mental reservations about the object of their devotions.

In another respect he was solitary. Although of Anglican and Conservative ancestry he became at an early age an enthusiastic devotee of Mr. Gladstone, and throughout his life he remained a staunch Liberal and Free Trader. But for the decline of his party he might have become an Elder Statesman, inheritor of the chaste laurels which had graced the brows of Lord Morley of Blackburn and Lord Bryce of Dechmont. But these two names recall the fact that Fisher had strayed into a camp where he could not always feel quite at ease; for Liberalism, when it is not of the North or West, Manchester, Scotland, Wales, is generally of the town, where it is most often connected with Dissent or Evangelicism, with rigid adherence to principles which Fisher himself considered illiberal. Gladstone, Rosebery and Grey, who had all been educated in the South, appeared to be members of that cultured world which had given Fisher birth, but with this important difference, that these three had the background and inheritance of the North, the first of Liverpool, the second of Midlothian, and the third of Northumberland, whereas Fisher pertained by temperament and circumstance to that cosmopolitan section of English society which from headquarters in the metropolis views the provinces as no more than a place for sport, or for occasional residence when the London season is over or Parliament is not in session. Fisher, representative of public school and residential university, was of that class of Englishman which has a state, and a home, but no *pays*, no provincial community which might have taken pride in his achievements, whose accent

he might have shared, however faintly, where he might constantly have renewed childhood memories, and to which he might
have turned for confirmation or even solace. By contrast, Liberalism
was strong in local attachment. And this sense of isolation was
deepened in proportion as his political colleagues died or drifted
away, so that politically Fisher was left with little more than his
principles, that form of solitude which only the strong-minded can
bear.

But if Fisher as a Liberal was somewhat anomalous, he was
without reserve an exponent of all that is best in our conception of
democracy. A democracy cannot work without efficient committees
and good chairmen, and to that extent he was a good democrat.
More important, no democracy can survive unless a minority is
prepared willingly to carry out a decision of the majority with
which it may be in disagreement, and Fisher answered to this strict
requirement. So too, if democracy implies forbearance, moderation,
willingness to live and let live, hatred of intolerance, cruelty and
superstition, and the retention by the subject of at least a part of
his individuality, then Fisher in practice as in theory was democratic.
Still more, if democracy means ' the determination to uphold the
cause of just and humane government at all times and in all circumstances, and to tolerate no falling short of their ethical standard,
on grounds of colour, race or nationality . . . to inscribe the sense
of trusteeship among the permanent conventions of the British
Empire,'[1] if, in other words, we can impose a high sense of personal
responsibility on both our citizenship and our statesmanship, we
can hail in Fisher not merely a good democrat but a great one. To
him these were the cardinal doctrines of Liberalism, but they had
already become the kernel of English public life, leaving the Liberal
Party no more than a shell.

As Rousseau found that ' liberty is not the fruit of every clime,'
so we have to recognise that a democracy such as Fisher's is not the
creation of a day. It was the achievement of centuries. No man
owed more to the past than did Fisher. His intelligence had first
been activated by Greek literature, in which he found beauty
identified not with the sensuous or the relaxing, but with the
qualities of balance, proportion and restraint; in Greek philosophy

[1] These words were used by Fisher of the Whigs—*The Whig Historians*, p. 30.

he admired the spirit of free enquiry, of intelligent curiosity, and in Plato he found that devotion to reason and truth which to him appeared the highest of the virtues. Ancient Rome embodied for him the virtues of patriotism, responsibility, discipline, the life ordered by the rule of service and law. The mediæval Holy Roman Empire stirred him as a half-conscious effort to restore in primitive conditions the unifying and civilising function of Imperial Rome, an ideal destined to succumb before the all-embracing activities of a great and highly-organised Church, which in giving to man a spiritual faith deprived him of a political opportunity. France provided another inspiration in Fisher's life. It was not the France of St. Louis or of St. Joan of Arc, of Pascal or of Lamartine, but the France which in its civilisation recalled the achievement of ancient Athens, austerely beautiful and almost feminine in its delicacy as in Racine; sceptical and iconoclastic as in Voltaire; half-amused and wholly saddened by human cruelty and folly as in Anatole France; or it might be France of the Revolution, of emancipation from injustice and obscurantism, of a new, secular gospel for the human race; or again it was the France of Napoleon, the chaos of unlimited conquest abroad, and the well-reasoned order of the *Code* at home. Nearer at hand in Fisher's life was England, so rich in poetry, in graceful survivals, in modulated progress, in social amenities, in the high and often idealist quality of its public life. These were among the old things which helped to make the modern democrat.

It was this subordination of the affective to the rational element, derived from the Platonic philosophy, which Fisher maintained so consistently as to give an impression of austerity and reserve. One of his very few confessions about himself was made to an intimate friend,[1] to whom he confided that in regard to Americans he felt himself spiritually akin to those Englishmen of Laud's day on account of whom the Puritans had been obliged to flee the country. This was an extraordinary admission by one who had proved such a personal success in the United States, the joy of American hostesses and the inspiration of Western audiences. In reality he was providing the real clue to his character—the rigorous and invariable subordination of his private to his public personality, a self-control so habitual that the two personalities were usually thought of as one;

---

[1] The late Sir Robert Rait.

and accordingly a sense of duty would often determine a course of conduct which might be at variance with his private predilection. Surely this is the climax of the democratic virtues, and obviously a nation of Fishers would need neither church, parliament nor police. But what at a distance looked like a public institution was often on closer inspection found to be a human being. Two instances may illustrate this. The first was in 1934, when he created such a favourable impression by his tact and eloquence at the Jacques Cartier celebrations in French Canada. On that occasion he received the congratulations of the Government and the Press; but what touched him most of all was a letter from the owner of a small and remote provision store,[1] warmly thanking him for his public assertion of the principle that the French Canadian could well combine his French civilisation with his Imperial loyalty. The second instance was in 1940. It was a request from a Negro school in the United States which had been visited by him. The schoolmistress, describing the confusion and doubt which the outbreak of war had brought to her charges, asked if he would send them some message, such as might help to confirm their sense of values. This request, perhaps the most genuine tribute ever paid to his influence over others, was never known by him, for the letter did not reach England until after his death.

In his later years, years of sorrow for all like himself who had lived and worked for high ideals, he maintained undiminished his hope of a brighter future for Europe:

'There is, despite the long and melancholy tale of European wars, a common foundation of European culture. Much of that precious inheritance the Germans, under their present leadership, renounce. But the Nazi fever will not infect the body politic for all time. The bad diplomatic tradition of the bumptious parvenu power working through perpetual menaces of war will break on the wheels of history, the fiery racialism will lose its appeal. . . . Other leaders will arise who will lay stress not on the hatefulness of Germany's neighbours, but upon the many things which the leading peoples of the world have in common. For we Europeans are more of a piece than the political fanatics would have us

[1] Monsieur Laurent Lacroix of Kenogami, September 17, 1934.

believe, and there are things less likely than that France and Britain will at last find a *modus vivendi* with the Germans and Italians who have helped with them to build up the fabric of European civilisation.'[1]

This was his last public pronouncement. It summed up for a Europe in dissolution all that might profitably be learned from the past, and in a time of deepening shadow it held out a distant gleam of hope.

[1] *The Fortnightly*, February, 1940.

Index

INDEX